There are a number of HORIZON CARAVEL BOOKS
published each year. Titles now available are:

BUILDING THE SUEZ CANAL
MOUNTAIN CONQUEST
PHARAOHS OF EGYPT
LEONARDO DA VINCI
THE FRENCH REVOLUTION
CORTES AND THE AZTEC CONQUEST
CAESAR
THE UNIVERSE OF GALILEO AND NEWTON
THE VIKINGS
MARCO POLO'S ADVENTURES IN CHINA

SHAKESPEARE'S ENGLAND
CAPTAIN COOK AND THE SOUTH PACIFIC
THE SEARCH FOR EARLY MAN
JOAN OF ARC
EXPLORATION OF AFRICA
NELSON AND THE AGE OF FIGHTING SAIL
ALEXANDER THE GREAT
RUSSIA UNDER THE CZARS
HEROES OF POLAR EXPLORATION
KNIGHTS OF THE CRUSADES

American Heritage also publishes AMERICAN HERITAGE JUNIOR LIBRARY
books, a similar series on American history. The titles now available are:

CAPTAINS OF INDUSTRY
CARRIER WAR IN THE PACIFIC
JAMESTOWN: FIRST ENGLISH COLONY
AMERICANS IN SPACE
ABRAHAM LINCOLN IN PEACE AND WAR
AIR WAR AGAINST HITLER'S GERMANY
IRONCLADS OF THE CIVIL WAR
THE ERIE CANAL
THE MANY WORLDS OF BENJAMIN FRANKLIN
COMMODORE PERRY IN JAPAN
THE BATTLE OF GETTYSBURG
ANDREW JACKSON, SOLDIER AND STATESMAN
ADVENTURES IN THE WILDERNESS
LEXINGTON, CONCORD AND BUNKER HILL
CLIPPER SHIPS AND CAPTAINS
D-DAY, THE INVASION OF EUROPE
THE STORY OF YANKEE WHALING

WESTWARD ON THE OREGON TRAIL
THE FRENCH AND INDIAN WARS
GREAT DAYS OF THE CIRCUS
STEAMBOATS ON THE MISSISSIPPI
COWBOYS AND CATTLE COUNTRY
TEXAS AND THE WAR WITH MEXICO
THE PILGRIMS AND PLYMOUTH COLONY
THE CALIFORNIA GOLD RUSH
PIRATES OF THE SPANISH MAIN
TRAPPERS AND MOUNTAIN MEN
MEN OF SCIENCE AND INVENTION
NAVAL BATTLES AND HEROES
THOMAS JEFFERSON AND HIS WORLD
DISCOVERERS OF THE NEW WORLD
RAILROADS IN THE DAYS OF STEAM
INDIANS OF THE PLAINS

A HORIZON CARAVEL BOOK

BUILDING THE
SUEZ CANAL

By the Editors of
HORIZON MAGAZINE

Author
S. C. BURCHELL

Consultant
CHARLES ISSAWI
Professor of Economics, Columbia University

Published by American Heritage Publishing Co., Inc.
Book Trade and Institutional Distribution by
Harper & Row

FIRST EDITION
Library of Congress Catalogue Card Number: 66–21551
©1966 by American Heritage Publishing Co., Inc., 551 Fifth Avenue, New York, New
York, 10017. All rights reserved under Berne and Pan-American Copyright Conventions.
Trademark CARAVEL registered United States Patent Office

FOREWORD

Men have exercised their courage and resourcefulness to win enduring fame in many different ways. Some have led armies to victory in mighty clashes involving thousands of soldiers. Others have followed lonely trails and crossed unknown waters to discover new lands. And today men are being hurled into space to explore far realms beyond the atmosphere of our planet. But not all the paths to glory are so dramatic.

Some men wage their battles against ignorance and prejudice, and they are heroes just as surely as are the generals, explorers, or spacemen. The story of one such quiet hero, Ferdinand de Lesseps, is told in *Building the Suez Canal*. Rulers, politicians, and financiers in Europe and in Egypt thought de Lesseps' ambitious scheme to link the waters of the Mediterranean and Red seas—thus cutting 5,800 miles off the India to Europe ocean voyage—was impractical, unwise, and even foolish. The hostile, empty desert of the Isthmus of Suez posed a seemingly insurmountable geographical challenge to the builder's ingenuity and persistence.

During the ten years of its construction, from 1859 to 1869, the Suez Canal was the focus of world-wide attention; many of the dramatic photographs, drawings, diagrams, maps, and etchings reproduced here are from the press of that period. Around the globe, people read about de Lesseps' progress much as they might follow campaigns in a war. Many were hoping for his defeat and humiliation; a few farsighted individuals realized that his final victory would be a triumph for mankind as well.

In the years since its completion, the Suez Canal has occasionally been the scene of conflict, as in the 1956 crisis in which Great Britain, France, and Israel stood on the brink of war with the United Arab Republic over possession of the waterway. But more frequently the hundred-mile-long channel has been the route of profitable commerce and peaceful travel between East and West, and has thus been a force for world unity. Today the startling sight of ships in the desert, as in the photograph opposite, is an enduring testimony to man's limitless vision and his ability to apply knowledge, skill, and will power toward the realization of his dreams.

THE EDITORS

The modern passenger ship Oriana, *of the Peninsular & Oriental line, appears to be plowing through great hills of sand. She is in fact sailing through the Suez Canal and was photographed from behind the canal embankment.*

RIGHT: *Basket-laden camels and donkeys carry sand away from the partially dug fresh-water canal.*
COMPAGNIE FINANCIERE DE SUEZ, PARIS

COVER: *An artist sketches the opening-day procession of ships as they move through the Suez Canal.*
COMPAGNIE FINANCIERE DE SUEZ, PARIS

FRONT ENDSHEET: *An Arab caravan on the El Qantara pier waits to be ferried across the new canal.*
COMPAGNIE FINANCIERE DE SUEZ, PARIS

TITLE PAGE: *In honor of the one hundred fiftieth anniversary of de Lesseps' birth, the canal company issued this gilded bronze medal.*
COLLECTION OF ROLAND DE LESSEPS

BACK ENDSHEET: *Two long jetties form an artificial harbor through which vessels pass en route from the Mediterranean to the canal.*
THE GRANGER COLLECTION

BACK COVER: *A gold box with a diamond monogram was a gift to de Lesseps from Khedive Ismail.*
COMPAGNIE FINANCIERE DE SUEZ, PARIS

CONTENTS

Seated on a palm-fringed dais (right) at Port Said, royal guests at the gala opening of the Suez Canal witness dual rites. On separate platforms Moslems (left) and Christians (center) give their individual benedictions.

I

CELEBRATION
IN THE DESERT

For a week now the vessels had been sailing into Port Said, Egypt's newest harbor, which lay on the Mediterranean side of the Isthmus of Suez. Today it was crowded with ships—nearly eighty of them riding at anchor in the calm water of the roadstead.

Some were yachts, some were merchant vessels, and some were men of war, all freshly decorated and painted for the occasion. Colorful pennants streamed from every mast, and the decks were lined with sailors in dress uniform. The flags of almost all the seafaring nations of the world fluttered in the light sea breeze. It was a clear, sparkling day under an intense blue sky.

At the front of the great flotilla rode a sleek black yacht that flew the colors of France. A few minutes before eight o'clock on this morning—Wednesday, November 17, 1869 —a beautiful woman appeared on the bridge of the yacht; with her was an older man in a black frock coat. Along the breakwaters and all around the curve of the harbor the crowd began to cheer. At the same time, cannon sounded from shore batteries and from all the warships lying at anchor. The stately woman smiled and waved her handkerchief, and the crowd roared again.

She was Eugénie, Empress of the French, and she had come all the way from Europe to be the guest of honor at this great celebration—the opening of the new Suez Canal. The man with her was Ferdinand de Lesseps, her cousin and the man who had developed the idea of the canal and built it—against great odds. Today the canal was a reality at last. It was a day, and a celebration, that promised to be one of the most splendid of the nineteenth century. Only a few months before, the Khedive Ismail, who ruled over Egypt, had personally delivered his invitation to Eugénie in Paris. Her attendance was the final touch to his magnifi-

The two reigning monarchs present at the canal opening were Empress Eugénie and Emperor Franz Josef.

cent plan for an event that the world would not soon forget.

Shielding her eyes against the bright Egyptian sun, Eugénie looked toward the shore. The cannon continued to fire, and the harbor was filling with smoke. But she could still make out the excited crowd.

There were Egyptian workers and soldiers, Bedouins and Turkish noblemen. There were Greek sailors and French engineers, merchants from Syria and veiled Tuaregs from the desert. There were black men from the Sudan and white men from all the countries of Europe—from England and Italy and Sweden, from France and Spain and Austria. Some had even come from Russia and the faraway Americas. Now they were crowded together around the harbor of Port Said, all anxious for a place near the water's edge. The great celebration was about to begin.

Eugénie's eyes sparkled. When she had left Marseilles almost two months earlier, she had not imagined that she would be sailing into an adventure out of *The Arabian Nights*.

But, during her journey, she ate strange foods and saw strange sights and heard strange sounds. She dined at Constantinople with the sultan of Turkey and his grand vizier. She lunched at a palace near the Great Pyramids with the Khedive himself. She saw Arab horsemen and Turkish lancers and savage tribesmen from the Congo. And she heard the cries of the bazaar and the Moslem prayers at sunset. Now, at last, she was beginning the most exciting part of her adventure. In a few minutes she would lead all the ships at Port Said through the magnificent new canal. For the next few days she would be at the center of all the mystery and magic and glamour of the Middle East.

Just before eight o'clock an unexpected silence fell over the harbor. The cannon stopped firing, and the crowd no longer cheered. There was only the faint cry of a seagull, and the clearest sound de Lesseps and the Empress could hear was the creaking of an anchor chain being raised. They nodded silently to each other, and de Lesseps took a watch from his pocket. The hands pointed to eight o'clock.

Then the silence in the harbor came to a sudden end. The air was filled with the hissing of steam whistles and the wailing of sirens. The cannon sounded again and again, and the crowd cheered with wilder excitement than before. Sailors shouted from the yardarms, and on the warships naval bands began to play. The stirring sound of military music filled the harbor.

With deafening blasts from her siren, *l'Aigle*, the yacht that carried de Lesseps and the Empress, started up. The

Eugénie and her companions stroll through the gardens that surround the palace of Gezireh, in Cairo, the sumptuous residence placed at the Empress' disposal by Ismail.

ship's paddle wheels churned the harbor water; then she moved ahead, veered slightly, and straightened out in order to enter the canal head on. The bands were playing a French military air called "Partant pour la Syrie" as the yacht passed through the entrance to the Suez Canal.

The incredible journey had begun. In front of the flotilla lay the hundred miles of silent desert that covers the Isthmus of Suez. But the desert had been conquered now, and the way was clear to the town of Suez itself—Suez, the miraculous new door that led to India and the riches of the Far East beyond.

At fifteen-minute intervals during the day, most of the other ships in the harbor entered the canal. They kept their speed to five knots an hour, and the distance between them was three quarters of a mile. In single file behind Eugénie's yacht came the *Greif*, which carried Emperor

The side-wheel steamer Greif *(center), carrying Emperor Franz Josef to the opening ceremonies of the Suez Canal, sails into Port Said harbor. Anchored vessels dressed with banners, their sailors lining the yards,*

greet the Austrian monarch with salvos. Some spectators attempt to get a closer view of the festivities by row-ing out toward the Greif, *while the crowds along the shore await a glimpse of the disembarking royal visitor.*

Franz Josef of Austria-Hungary and his party, a frigate with the Crown Prince of Prussia, and at the appropriate interval, a Dutch yacht with the Prince and Princess of Holland on board. They were in turn followed by a Russian ship with the Grand Duke Michael and General Ignatiev, who came as representatives of the czar. The *Psyche* steamed by, and at the railing was the British ambassador to Constantinople. One after another nearly fifty of the ships in the harbor turned into the Suez Canal. Not since the days of the pharaohs had so much activity been seen on this barren isthmus in a remote corner of Egypt.

The day passed, and *l'Aigle* steamed slowly through the canal at the head of the great international procession. The desert was astonishingly beautiful. A British colonel, watching from the deck of one of the merchant ships, said later that it was "an enchanted scene." And surely it must have seemed like some fantastic mirage, with silent ships floating on the desert and white-robed Bedouins watching from the banks of the canal.

By five in the afternoon, less than ten hours after leaving Port Said, the first ships were approaching Ismailia. Just before six o'clock in the evening, the yacht carrying de Lesseps and the Empress steamed into Lake Timsah.

This lake forms a perfect natural harbor, and while the canal was being dug, workmen had built a handsome town on the lake's northwest shore. They called it Ismailia in honor of the Khedive of Egypt. It marked the approximate half-way point between Port Said on the Mediterranean and Suez on a gulf of the Red Sea and was an ideal place to regroup and prepare for the rest of the journey.

More than this, Ismailia was an ideal place for the Khedive Ismail to give a party. He had turned his namesake into an elaborate stage setting of Eastern splendor. It was a fairyland of flowers and lights and ornate buildings that might have come from the pages of an Oriental adventure story. The Khedive was a grandiose ruler who loved nothing better than luxury and ostentation. This was the great moment of his life, his chance for immortality, and he spared no expense on the decoration of Ismailia. The cost of his fabulous party, in fact, came to some seven and a half million dollars. On Wednesday night, while his guests slept on their yachts in the harbor, the Khedive roamed the many rooms of his magnificent palace, arranging the last details of the next day's festivities. All through the night, torches flickered along the docks and in the streets of Ismailia, and the lights in the palace burned until dawn.

Crown Prince Frederick of Prussia

Princess Sophia of Holland

Prince Henry of Holland

On Thursday morning, November 18, the good weather held, and the sky was bright and clear once again. The harbor of Ismailia presented an even more vivid spectacle than Port Said had the day before. All along the shore flagpoles had been set up, and the banners of crimson and gold —some with crosses and others with Moslem crescents— furled and unfurled in the soft breeze. The Khedive's palace, gleaming in the sunlight, stood near the lake and dominated the town. There were flowers everywhere and triumphal arches and green trees. Early in the morning the warships began firing their cannon, and the sirens and the whistles began again. The harbor, like Port Said, was a sea of masts, flags, and drifting smoke.

Before noon, to the delight of the crowd on the dock, a launch brought Ferdinand de Lesseps and the Empress to shore. Dressed in yellow and wearing a large straw hat with a flowing veil, Eugénie was a strange and lovely sight in the middle of the desert. A Bedouin guard, in red cloaks and mounted on white camels, escorted the Empress and her party to a picnic on the outskirts of town.

After lunch they returned to the dock, where Emperor Franz Josef and other dignitaries were waiting. They all stepped into their carriages and drove away through a tree-lined boulevard between two rows of Egyptian cavalry— one regiment of lancers on white horses and another mounted on bays. They passed through streets of luxurious private houses and under huge shade trees. They saw flowers on every side of them and admired the lovely gardens in the Place Champollion. At last their carriage reached the desert plain outside Ismailia.

Here there was an enormous Arab encampment, for the Khedive had invited, in addition to his European guests, some thirty thousand Arabs to the great celebration. They had put up their gaily striped tents in the desert outside of town, and they had brought with them their wives, their children, their flocks of sheep, and their camels. Now they wished to repay the Khedive's generosity by putting on a show for his European guests.

Eugénie, de Lesseps, and Emperor Franz Josef took their places with the others under the awning of a sumptuous tent. Luxurious rugs lay on the sand under their feet, and brass trays on wooden stands held coffee, dates, and other delicacies. The Arab chieftains were all dressed in hoods and flowing capes of soft white wool, and at their waists they carried gleaming daggers of Damascus steel. Suddenly, one of the chieftains raised his arm in a signal.

17

At once the flat sandy plain in front of the tent was filled with Arab horsemen. They galloped past, with burnooses flying in the wind and carbines firing as they went. Great clouds of dust rolled up and slowly settled, and then there were wild dervishes from the Sudan—some holding red-hot coals between their teeth and others swallowing live scorpions. Next, fakirs took their turn with tricks of magic. The entertainment went on far into the afternoon as the day passed in a whirl of color and excitement.

By nightfall, fireworks had started in the harbor of Ismailia. The ships at anchor were strung with lights of every color, and Chinese lanterns and torches gleamed on the shore. At intervals rockets rose into the air, and small stars exploded in the sky. It seemed to one observer as if "the heavens were on fire." Certainly the harbor itself was a blaze of light.

And so was the town of Ismailia. Lights were shining on every street, and they all seemed to be leading in the direction of the Khedive's palace. At last the time had come for the party to begin. The Khedive had invited more than four thousand guests from Europe to celebrate the opening of the Suez Canal. In order to entertain them in the proper style, he had built this magnificent palace in less than six months' time. It was surrounded with lush gardens and a pavilion where nearly a thousand people could sit down to dinner. The palm trees in front were hung with innumerable lanterns.

Inside, the palace was equally splendid. All the furniture had been ordered from Paris, and crystal chandeliers

The back of a camel provides Empress Eugénie with a clear view of an equestrian performance by Arab horsemen (above). Emperor Franz Josef indulges in a more strenuous form of sightseeing. At left, he is being helped to climb a pyramid's giant step.

dazzled the eye in every room. Gilt chairs and marble-topped tables were everywhere, and costly paintings from France hung upon the walls. There were a thousand waiters in scarlet liveries and powdered wigs. In the vast kitchens five hundred cooks were preparing a feast of wild duck, pheasant, and partridge.

The town of Ismailia had a carnival air. All the streets that led to the palace were overflowing with people, and there were dancers and jugglers and musicians on every

19

A parade of carriages led by Empress Eugénie and Emperor Franz Josef moves across the desert outside Ismailia. Driving his own phaeton, the Khedive (right foreground) escorts the party. In the distance is Ismail's new palace.

corner. Those lucky enough to have been invited to the party could hardly get through the crowds.

In the palace itself there was even greater confusion. The rooms were crowded to the point of suffocation, since all of the thousands of guests seemed to be arriving at once. An orchestra played, but there was no room to dance. Buffet tables were weighted with nearly every delicacy the world could offer, but no one could get near them. Waiters passed champagne on silver trays, but it was difficult to reach the glasses. Those who did were scarcely able to raise them to their lips.

Still the guests arrived, and now the walls of the palace seemed to bulge. Each room was a riot of color, and each room, by itself, was a miniature portrait of the world as a whole. For the Khedive's guests had come from every country under the sun, and they were dressed in every costume imaginable.

Diamonds, rubies, and sapphires gleamed in the candlelight, and so did military decorations and silver swords and the jeweled handles of scimitars. The uniforms and costumes were wonderful to see. There were diplomats and naval officers and military men from all the countries of the world. There were beautiful women dressed in costumes of the East, and from Europe there were ladies wearing the latest Parisian fashions.

At midnight the Empress Eugénie arrived, more lovely than ever. A diamond coronet glittered in her black hair, and her gown was dazzling. She sat with the Khedive and Emperor Franz Josef, and together they toasted the success of the Suez Canal. They drank to France and to Egypt. They drank to peace, to international harmony, and to the future of the world.

But, strangely enough, all eyes in the room were not on the glamorous royal party. Most of them were turned in the direction of a quiet man in black evening clothes. For Ferdinand de Lesseps had been the center of attention ever since the moment he appeared on the bridge of the im-

Illustrated London News

Bedouins camped outside Ismailia pass an evening playing native musical instruments and smoking their hookahs. European visitors (far left) are being guided around the quarters by a Bedouin sheik.

21

perial yacht and the great adventure had neared its climax.

Yet he wore no elegant uniform, and his dark clothes made him seem somewhat out of place in this exotic company. But, one by one, the Khedive's guests came up to him, and he heard words of praise in every language. A crowd closed in around him, and before long the plain black figure was lost in a many-colored sea of silk, velvet, and satin.

It was strange, for he did not have Eugénie's glamour or the Khedive's sense of style. He was not young, nor was

he handsome. An Englishman who attended the party that night described him as short and lithe and neat, with "hair as white as snow, a complexion clear and red as a rosy apple, dark flashing eyes, and a black mustache." Certainly he seemed more like a kindly village grandfather than the mighty builder of the Suez Canal and the man his contemporaries were to call the Great Frenchman.

However, this splendid evening—indeed, the whole fantastic celebration—in some ways belonged to him alone. He had given nearly his entire life to the creation of the

Royal visitors being rowed across the harbor at Suez get an enthusiastic send-off from spectators on a jetty. Imperial yachts, already under steam, line the harbor quay.

Suez Canal and had had the incredible strength to turn a young man's dream into reality. He had created a green world in the middle of the desert. Only a short while ago there had been no magnificent palace at Ismailia. There had been little water and no trees and no flowers. There had been no towns and no harbors. There had been nothing but the endless desert. Surely, without him, there would have been no party that night. Without him there would have been no canal at all.

But his road to the palace at Ismailia had not been an easy one. It had been a long road, and he had traveled it almost alone. Now, this evening, he was a hero at last. Only two days before, at a religious ceremony in Port Said, he had been compared to Christopher Columbus. The comparison was not greatly exaggerated. For, like Columbus, Ferdinand de Lesseps—in creating the Suez Canal—had opened up a whole new world. He had joined the East and the West, and he had made two separate halves of the world into one. The long and dangerous ocean voyage around the Cape of Good Hope could now be avoided.

In an elegant atmosphere of palms and elaborate candelabras, distinguished guests relax between one of the twenty-four courses served at the Khedive's banquet in Ismailia.

Europe could obtain the treasures of the Orient at far less cost; greater trade and prosperity would almost inevitably develop. De Lesseps had spent many long years in bringing all this about, and that night, at the Khedive Ismail's party, honor and recognition came to him at last. It was only the beginning.

In a little while he would read a simple and dramatic announcement in London's *Shipping Gazette*: "As far as we are concerned, we can only point to the fact that the French engineers have redeemed their promise. The canal is open and is a magnificent success." And in a few days he would read with an ironic smile a letter from Lord Clarendon, the British Foreign Secretary: "Notwithstanding the obstacles of every kind against which you have had to contend, and which were the necessary result both of physical circumstance and of a local state of society to which such undertakings were unknown and where the removal of difficulties depended on your own genius and resource, a brilliant success has finally rewarded your indomitable perseverance." Lord Clarendon neglected to mention that England had been responsible for most of these difficulties.

Before long de Lesseps would have more material rewards. He would receive the Grand Cross of the Legion of Honor from Eugénie and the Grand Cordon of the Order of Osmanie from the Khedive of Egypt. Napoleon III, Emperor of the French, would offer to make him Duke of Suez, and he would be entertained by Queen Victoria of England, whose government had once been his greatest enemy. In London, Paris, and New York he would be the idol of the day.

That evening, in the Khedive's palace, he was enjoying his first moments of glory. Truly his accomplishment had been a magnificent one. On a barren desert he had built one of the great highways of the world. He had brought the Mediterranean and the Red Sea together, and he had organized a peaceful international undertaking. He had created a work of genius, but he had paid a tremendous price for it.

De Lesseps was sixty-four years old in 1869, and it had taken him almost half a lifetime to cross the hundred sandy miles from Port Said to Suez. And he had learned, at great cost to himself, something of the indifference of the world and the vulnerability of a dream.

The journey had been long from the beginning of his dream to the realization of it. It had been long, and it had been brutal.

Her journey through the canal completed, Eugénie is rowed to shore (the boat with the awning) at Suez. A triumphal arch forms a backdrop for the last leg of her trip.

II

THE DREAM

The journey began for Ferdinand de Lesseps—as it ended —in Egypt. Although the end was all sound and color and triumph, the beginning came quietly and without fanfare.

It came on an afternoon in 1832—nearly forty years before the November day on which a French yacht carried him through the completed Suez Canal. That afternoon in 1832 found de Lesseps, then a young man of twenty-seven, in a hospital at Alexandria. This seaport was Egypt's main gateway to the Mediterranean, and de Lesseps had just arrived to take up his new post as French vice-consul. By now he had expected to be hard at work in the consulate. Certainly he had not expected to be in a hospital, looking out in frustration at the harbor of Alexandria.

He was bored and angry and restless. Flies circled around his head, and the room was growing hot and uncomfortable. Through the window he could see the ship that had brought him from Tunis the day before. The long voyage on the *Diogenes* had been miserable enough. But shortly before they reached Alexandria, a passenger had died of what the ship's doctor called cholera. It made little difference that the diagnosis was wrong; for the present, de Lesseps and the other passengers found themselves under quarantine.

The flies were maddening now, and the afternoon was growing hotter and more and more uncomfortable. The confinement was especially difficult for an impatient young man like de Lesseps who had, as one friend put it, "unflagging energy." For the past few years he had been following his family's tradition of service in the diplomatic corps. His father had been French consul at Tunis, and he himself had been vice-consul there and apprentice consul at Lisbon. Now he was anxious to get on with his career. This quarantine, however, had tied his hands completely.

Ferdinand de Lesseps, fashionably attired in a tropical suit, gazes from the window of his Alexandria quarters toward the Mediterranean Sea. In this water-color portrait of the builder during his 1832–37 consulship, he seems lost in thought, his book and telescope laid aside, daydreaming of canals.

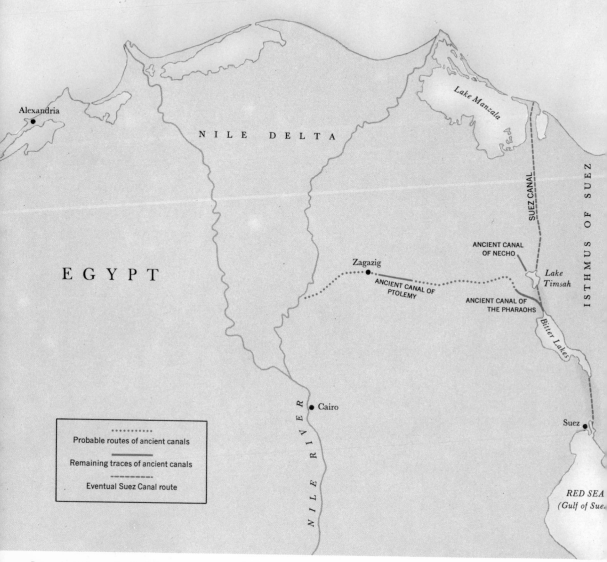

MEDITERRANEAN SEA

Alexandria

NILE DELTA

Lake Manzala

EGYPT

SUEZ CANAL

ISTHMUS OF SUEZ

Zagazig

ANCIENT CANAL OF PTOLEMY

ANCIENT CANAL OF NECHO

Lake Timsah

ANCIENT CANAL OF THE PHARAOHS

Bitter Lakes

Cairo

NILE RIVER

• • • • • • • • • •
Probable routes of ancient canals

Remaining traces of ancient canals

Eventual Suez Canal route

Suez

RED SEA (Gulf of Suez)

In ancient times the Red Sea may have reached far inland from Suez (shaded area). Receding waters left the depressions of the Bitter Lakes and Lake Timsah. The route of the pharaohs' canal followed an impression left by an easterly flowing Nile tributary, which by pharaonic times had filled with silt.

There was little for him to do but brood about his own troubles. He felt trapped and forgotten and miserably alone.

So, he was more than delighted when late in the afternoon he received an unexpected visitor. It was his superior, the French consul general, and he had brought along an armful of books to relieve the young man's boredom. It was a gesture of remarkable consequences.

For among the books the consul general brought were several volumes of the *Description de l'Egypte*. This was a

28

work that had been compiled by scholars and scientists attached to the French army that invaded Egypt under Napoleon's command in 1798. It was a fascinating book in itself and would prove especially so for young Ferdinand de Lesseps. The *Description de l'Egypte* marked the turning point of his life and signaled the beginning of his dream.

When the consul general had gone, de Lesseps, eager now for any diversion, picked up a volume and began to read at random. With this casual gesture—and without knowing it—he had taken the first step along a road he would follow with growing enthusiasm for the next forty years. It was a road that would meet him at every turning with obstacles of the most discouraging kind. It was the long road to Suez.

Years later, he remembered that the dream of a canal through the Isthmus of Suez "had taken possession of my imagination after reading the report of Lepère, the head engineer in the expedition of General Bonaparte." By chance, the volume he selected that afternoon in Alexandria had as its subject the isthmus. It contained the report of a survey of the area made by Lepère during the French occupation of 1798–1801.

De Lesseps was unfamiliar with that part of Egypt—in fact, with any part of the country at all. He only knew that the Isthmus of Suez was a narrow neck of land at the eastern border of Egypt, lying between the delta of the Nile and the Sinai Peninsula and separating the Mediterranean from the Red Sea. It was little more than a hundred miles wide. And he had heard too that it was a forbidding desert inhabited only by a handful of nomadic Bedouin tribesmen. He knew little else, but his knowledge grew as he turned the pages of Lepère's report.

He learned that Napoleon had sent Lepère to the isthmus in order to explore the possibility of digging a canal through it. By joining the Mediterranean to the Red Sea a once-important trade route to the Far East could be opened again. Such a feat would add greatly to the glory—and to the profit—of France. In fact, France's Republican rulers had given Napoleon specific orders to initiate such a canal and re-establish French trade with the Orient. Napoleon considered it so important that he went himself to the isthmus late in 1798. Lepère was impressed with the interest the general took in the survey and with his desire to have the "most exact information." As ordered, Lepère continued his explorations. After long study, he decided that a canal between the Mediterranean and the Red Sea would

Napoleon in Egypt, with plumes in his tricorne hat, invests an Arab sheik with a shawl of Republican red, white, and blue colors.

ANCIENT
WATERWAYS

In building canals across the desert to the Suez area, the pharaohs were following the lead of prehistoric geography— the Nile at one time had been connected with the Red Sea (see map on page 28). When they retraced this route, the Egyptians gained access to the rich copper mines of the Sinai Peninsula and the spice lands of East Africa. The Egyptian ship opposite, above, is being loaded at Punt (possibly modern Somalia) with the myrrh trees much coveted in the land of the pharaohs. After the Persian conquest of Egypt in the sixth century B.C., Darius (left, above, on a relief at his capital at Persepolis) reopened the canal that had fallen into disuse during the decline of the pharaohs and had filled with silt. The waterway became a vital communication link between Persepolis and Darius' African provinces. Although Egypt was relegated to the status of a colony during the Roman occupation, the Emperor Trajan saw the value of imitating the pharaohs. With an Egyptian canal system he could carry troops and goods from the Mediterranean Sea to the Red Sea and thus insure the growth and prosperity of Rome. Puteoli (opposite), a great Roman port in southern Italy, was often crowded with ships bringing cargoes from North Africa. Today, traces of ancient canals (at left) can still be seen in the Egyptian desert.

be impossible. He based this opinion on the mistaken belief that there was a thirty-foot difference in water level between them.

Yet Lepère did dwell on the fact that he had found in the desert many traces of an ancient canal—a canal that had once led from the Nile at Zagazig to the Gulf of Suez. He saw a possibility of rebuilding the canal, since it provided a path to the Mediterranean by way of the Nile. It was the lost canal of the pharaohs.

For de Lesseps the name alone was a romantic echo of the Egyptian past. Long after the quarantine at Alexandria was over and he was busy at the consulate, he often thought of that vanished canal. And he often thought of the Isthmus of Suez itself and the great wall of sand it put between Europe and the Orient. The ancient history of the isthmus began to fascinate him, and soon he had turned it into a hobby to fill his free hours. At Alexandria and at Cairo, where he was later sent, he searched the libraries for more books to read and more maps to study.

According to some scholars the canal of the pharaohs had been built by the rulers of Egypt two thousand years before the birth of Christ. It had been started by the Pharaoh Sesostris I in the Twelfth Dynasty (1991–1786 B.C.) but did not go directly from sea to sea. The canal cut across from the Pelusiac branch of the Nile, north of present-day Cairo, to the two Bitter Lakes, which in turn led to the Gulf of Suez.

It was a narrow canal but sufficient for the ships of that age, which could sail along the Nile from the Mediterranean Sea and then proceed by canal to the Red Sea. It was a well-traveled route, and with few interruptions, continued to be followed until the Twenty-sixth Dynasty (664–525 B.C.)—some twelve hundred years later. By then desert winds had piled sand beyond the Bitter Lakes, blocking the way to the Gulf of Suez and the Red Sea. The Pharaoh Necho tried to excavate a new channel, but more than one hundred thousand workers—according to one ancient account—died in the unsuccessful attempt. Darius, King of Persia (522–485 B.C.), made an effort to put this part of the canal back into working order. And finally it was extended all the way to Arsinoë—the modern port of Suez—by Ptolemy II (283–246 B.C.).

During the Roman occupation of Egypt the canal of the pharaohs was maintained and improved, particularly by the Emperor Trajan (A.D. 98–117). When the Romans left, however, it was allowed to deteriorate. In the seventh cen-

Lepère (above), who surveyed the isthmus during Napoleon's occupation, believed it was possible to rebuild the canal of the pharaohs.

tury, at the time of the Moslem domination of Egypt, it was rebuilt by order of the Caliph Omar. The canal remained in use for another century, and then the desert claimed it again. It was no longer needed as a route for conquest, and trade could move overland; so the canal lay buried for more than a thousand years—its existence known only to wandering Arabs until Lepère's 1798 discovery.

The strange fate of the canal of the pharaohs fascinated de Lesseps. And one question continued to puzzle him: why had Egyptian pharaohs and Roman emperors and Moslem caliphs made so many attempts to open a waterway between the Mediterranean and the Red Sea?

The answer, he eventually determined, was a simple one. In ancient times the Isthmus of Suez had been the site of one of the world's great military and trade routes. Egypt stood then, as she does now, at the crossroad of two worlds. And Suez was the gate that opened from the West into Arabia, India, and all the nations of the Far East.

A look at history proved the point. De Lesseps discovered that during the Roman occupation of Egypt, for example, the Isthmus of Suez had been the scene of the land's greatest commercial activity. At that time a flourishing trade existed between the Eastern and the Western worlds. Greek and Arab merchants passed daily over the desert, both by ship on the canal and overland in great caravans. They carried one luxury after another to exchange for the gold and merchandise of the Roman Empire.

Napoleon's expedition popularized the study of Egyptian antiquities. At right, Count de Forbin, a compatriot of Napoleon's, poses while measuring the head of a sphinx.

Marco Polo's round-trip journey overland to the Orient lasted from 1271 to 1295. At left is the famous merchant's portrait, from a fifteenth-century manuscript of his travels. Two hundred years after Marco Polo, in 1498, Vasco da Gama (below), in a ten-month voyage around the Cape of Good Hope, discovered a new route to the East.

They brought tigers from the Punjab and leopards from Afghanistan, wool from Kashmir and silk from China, furs from Tibet and sapphires from Ceylon, incense from Yemen, and spices from the islands of Southeast Asia. They brought all the riches of the East across the sand from Suez to Alexandria. And from this busy seaport the goods were sent on to Rome and the faraway cities of the empire.

Even after the canal of the pharaohs was abandoned under the caliphs, merchants still crossed the desert by caravan. For six hundred years they were met at Alexandria by Italian and French ships that carried the merchandise on to Venice and Marseilles and the rest of Europe. But during this time a new route to the Far East had been discovered. In 1271 Marco Polo traveled through Persia to China on the northern overland route, which came to be used extensively during the fourteenth and fifteenth centuries. This route competed with the Suez caravans and took a good deal of trade from them.

More serious competition came in 1498, when a Portuguese explorer sailed to India around the Cape of Good Hope. Vasco da Gama, by rounding the tip of Africa, had found a new way to the Far East. His route was much longer, but it had a number of advantages over the Isthmus of Suez. Safety was its greatest virtue, for it put an end to the danger of Arab raiders in the desert and pirates in the Red Sea as well as eliminating the hazards of navigation in the narrow Red Sea and Gulf of Suez. More than this, the new route bypassed the Ottoman Empire and completely avoided the barrier the Turks had placed between Europe and the Orient.

So, at the end of the fifteenth century, the Egyptian link in the great chain of trade with the East was broken. The Venetians proposed reopening the canal route in the sixteenth century, but they and the French soon lost their Oriental commerce. It fell into the hands of the English, the Dutch, and the Portuguese, who sailed their merchant fleets around the Cape of Good Hope. The sun burned down on the Isthmus of Suez, and the desert was silent for four hundred years.

By 1833, when de Lesseps was made French consul at Cairo, daring travelers were already making the trip across the desert. Naturally, with his new interest in the subject, de Lesseps talked to them. Their reports were not enthusiastic. The Isthmus of Suez was a wasteland, nearly forgotten at the edge of Egypt. The only signs of life were cranes and flamingos and a few fishermen on the shores of

Until the completion of the canal in 1869, Suez remained a sleepy Arab town; only turbaned Bedouins waiting for ferries populate the harbor of Suez in this water

color by Louis Crapelet. Ferdinand de Lesseps, during a tour of the Isthmus of Suez in 1854, described the town as "a mere point [of land] surrounded by deserts."

Lake Manzala. Occasionally, there was the black tent of a Bedouin. The canal had vanished, and the Bitter Lakes were dry.

All that de Lesseps heard depressed him enormously. The romantic and productive past of the isthmus—from the canal of the pharaohs to the great desert caravans—made a strange contrast with its melancholy isolation in the 1830's. During his five years in Cairo, de Lesseps grew more and more convinced that something could and should be done. And he dreamed of reopening through Suez a path of communication between the people of the Eastern and Western worlds. To reactivate the great trade route, there should be another canal of the pharaohs, this time leading from sea to sea. He had finally come to focus his mind on the creation of a new canal.

Later in life, de Lesseps could never really explain it—how or when he reached a point where the canal had become the fabric of a dream. Yet he did say, in a letter to an old friend in 1852, that "piercing the Isthmus of Suez [was] ... a question which I had already been considering when we first made acquaintance with each other in Egypt twenty years ago." It was a young man's dream, visionary and impractical.

Oddly enough, it happened that Cairo in the 1830's was an ideal place for a young man with thoughts about canal building. True, not many people were interested in the deserted Isthmus of Suez, but de Lesseps was by no means the only person in Egypt who had notions of building a canal through the desert.

One morning in 1833 a most unusual visitor came through the doors of the French consulate in Cairo. The task of seeing him fell to de Lesseps. His superior, the consul general, did not feel quite up to it; de Lesseps soon understood why.

Looking up from his desk, de Lesseps studied with interest his caller, Prosper Enfantin, who was a strange figure, to say the least. He was dressed entirely in white and wore a long flowing robe with a wide sash. This was remarkable enough, but he also wore a shirt with the words *Le Père* ("Father") embroidered on it. This costume was odd even for Cairo, where the exotic was taken for granted.

Unfortunately, as Enfantin explained to the young consul, he had a small problem. Being a French citizen, he felt entitled to seek help at the consulate. He went on to say that he had somehow offended Mohammed Ali, Viceroy of Egypt, and had been asked to leave the country. Perhaps

Canal booster Prosper Enfantin wears, as part of his outlandish costume, a shirt labeled with the words Le Père *("Father"), the title that proclaims his exalted status among the Saint-Simonians.*

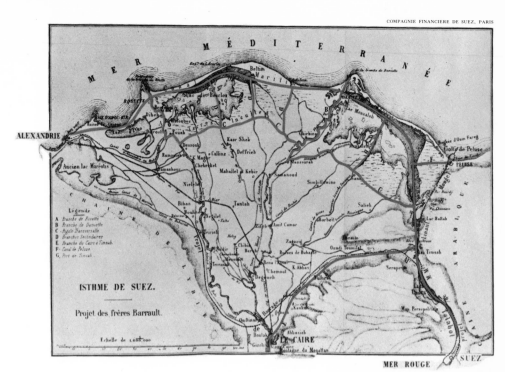

One of many plans submitted for a canal system in Egypt was drawn up by the Barrault brothers. This project, supported by Enfantin, included major canals connecting "Caire" with Lake Timsah and Suez with "Alexandrie". Other lines indicate smaller waterways.

Monsieur de Lesseps would have some solution to this difficulty?

By good luck, Enfantin had come to the right person. De Lesseps was a popular figure at the Egyptian court and had a certain amount of influence there. Years before, his father had served as consul in Egypt and had developed a close friendship with Mohammed Ali. Now de Lesseps was on particularly good terms with the Viceroy's son, Prince Mohammed Said, then a boy of eleven. Certainly de Lesseps was in a position to help his eccentric countryman. And he was more than pleased to do so, once he had heard Enfantin's story.

His reason for being in Egypt was bound to interest de Lesseps, for it concerned a projected canal through the Isthmus of Suez. Enfantin had just arrived in Cairo with twenty of his disciples and several engineers. He was the leader of a French philosophical group known as the Saint-Simonians. Their humanitarian impulses were strong, and they had been working on a number of ideas designed to bring the people of the world closer together. Among these ideas were proposals for two canals—one at the Isthmus of Panama and the other at the Isthmus of Suez. Enfantin, who had written many articles on the subject of a canal, had come to Egypt to interest the Viceroy in the idea. Mo-

Within the massive walls of Cairo's Citadel, Mohammed Ali slaughtered his adversaries the Mamelukes in 1811, making himself the undisputed ruler of Egypt. This 1857 lithograph depicts the Citadel from the unpaved public square below. From inside the walls the alabaster minarets and clustered domes of the mosque of Mohammed Ali rise above the city. The history of the mosque is as violent as that of its builder. In 1824 it was blown up; but by 1857 it had been rebuilt by Mohammed Ali's son, Mohammed Said.

hammed Ali, however, was opposed to such a project, fearing that the proposed waterway would make Egypt a mere pawn in power struggles among the European nations. "I don't want another Bosporus," he is reported to have said in reference to the natural water link between the Black Sea and the Mediterranean, which over the centuries had brought innumerable wars and intrigue to Turkey. Moreover, the Viceroy was anxious to have these visionaries out of his country. Their plans for a canal were annoying enough, but in addition Enfantin and his followers had odd symbolic ideas about the project being a marriage between East and West.

De Lesseps was more sympathetic. He was able to overlook the strange costume and the mystical ideas and see in Enfantin a man like himself—a man interested in building a canal through Suez. In a way de Lesseps came to admire him, and he finally persuaded Mohammed Ali to let him stay on in Egypt.

Two years later, in 1835, an enterprising Englishman came out of the desert. His name was Thomas Waghorn, and he had spent a great deal of time on the Isthmus of Suez. A former British naval lieutenant who had served in India, he had long been familiar with Suez and the Red Sea area. After resigning his commission, Waghorn became an agent for the East India Company in Cairo. His company was gradually coming to the conclusion that the long voyage from India to England around the Cape of Good Hope was too expensive and too impractical. Waghorn was convinced of it. He felt that the only path between East and West lay across the Isthmus of Suez.

He had been out in the desert, much to everyone's amusement, trying to re-establish the great overland caravan route from Suez to Cairo. In 1835 he began a passenger and mail service by coach across the desert. A few years later he merged his operations with another firm that owned a hotel at Suez for travelers from the Orient and several inns at halting places along the way to Cairo. Although Waghorn's interest in such a remote travel route was generally ignored, de Lesseps was quick to see the man's importance as a pioneer of the overland route. In fact, at the opening of the Suez Canal in 1869, de Lesseps insisted that a statue be erected in honor of Waghorn. And he was generous enough to declare: "He opened the route. We followed."

In the Cairo of the 1830's, men such as Waghorn and Enfantin were considered hopelessly impractical and even

Thomas Waghorn, pioneer of the overland route, was one of the first men to realize the importance of a path across the Isthmus of Suez.

a little mad. Under these circumstances it was fortunate that de Lesseps had at the time a good friend who was sane and practical—and who also happend to be interested in the idea of a canal. He was Adolphe Linant de Bellefonds, consulting engineer and irrigation adviser to the Egyptian government. A Frenchman, Linant Bey (as he was known in Egypt) was very familiar with the topography of the Isthmus of Suez. He had been in the country since 1818 and was precisely the steadying influence that de Lesseps needed. They often talked of the canal. Linant Bey, with his practical knowledge, convinced de Lesseps that the construction of the canal was a technical possibility. Years later, he headed the engineering team that de Lesseps sent out to Suez when the great project had at last begun.

The five years he spent in Cairo gave de Lesseps many chances to satisfy his growing curiosity about a Suez canal. He devoted a great deal of time to the idea—invaluable time, as it later turned out. Nevertheless, he was still a member of the French consular service and had many other responsibilities. The inevitable day came when his career called him away from Egypt. In 1837 he was transferred from Cairo. He was not to see the city again for almost twenty years.

His future did not seem to lie in the Middle East after all. An ambitious young man, de Lesseps traveled on from post to post—to The Hague and to Rotterdam, to Málaga, Barcelona, and Madrid, and then to Rome. Soon he married and raised a family. As time passed, he became totally absorbed in his profession, and the role of diplomat seemed to be one for which he was well suited. His manner was perfect for it; as one friend said, he was "cordial without fulsomeness, frank without familiarity, friendly without suspicion of insincerity." He had every social grace and was, in addition, a fine horseman, a crack shot, and an accomplished dancer. A young man of this kind would naturally rise in the French diplomatic service. Moreover, he had a fine record—performing splendidly in such difficult situations as the cholera epidemic of 1835 in Cairo and at Barcelona during the revolution of 1842.

The years followed one another. They were years full of

Egypt in the time of Mohammed Ali was renowned for breeding Arab horses. Opposite, the bearded ruler and his entourage ride prancing steeds against a romanticized backdrop. His pride in the breed led him to commission George Henry Laporte, a famous animal painter, to portray him in the saddle.

After leaving the diplomatic service, de Lesseps and his family retired to La Chênaie (the Oak Grove), an estate in the Berry region in central France. The turreted château had once been the hunting lodge of King Charles VII.

activity and the responsibilities of job and family. Egypt and the desert and a Suez canal faded farther and farther into the back of his mind. Surely, when he thought of it at all, the canal must have seemed to him no more than a young man's impossible dream.

Yet Ferdinand de Lesseps had by no means forgotten the canal. Over the years he kept up a correspondence with an old friend who was still in Cairo—S. W. Ruyssenaers, the Dutch consul general. Ruyssenaers wrote often, describing the latest developments on the Isthmus of Suez. De Lesseps learned that Linant Bey had made a survey in 1840 and had proof that the canal was technically possible to build. De Lesseps had also been in touch with Prosper Enfantin. In 1846 that strange philosopher had

44

gone so far as to form a society for the study of the canal (the Société d'Etudes) and in the following year had sent a team of European surveyors into the desert. They had corrected the error of Napoleon's engineer, Lepère, reporting that there was practically no difference in water level between the Mediterranean and the Red Sea.

Nor was the overland route pioneered by Waghorn being neglected. By 1845 the Bombay-to-London mail was being delivered in thirty days (as against four months around the tip of Africa), and two thousand passengers a year were being transported across the Isthmus of Suez. De Lesseps realized that these were all significant developments toward the eventual building of a canal. But he felt more and more removed from the whole idea. His life seemed to be taking an entirely different direction.

COMPAGNIE FINANCIERE DE SUEZ, PARIS

S. W. Ruyssenaers

Then, one day in 1849, his career in the diplomatic service came to a sudden end. As a special envoy to Rome, he had countermanded some orders sent by the French government. He was recalled to Paris and severely reprimanded. Actually, he had done nothing wrong; rather, he was a victim of the politics and incompetence of Louis Napoleon's government. In anger, de Lesseps resigned. He was only forty-four years old, and his career as a diplomat was over. He cast about for something else to do, and for want of a better solution he went into retirement in France, taking over the management of his mother-in-law's estate, La Chênaie, in the Berry region.

For the moment he seemed content to stay in this rustic backwater and play the part of a gentleman farmer. Egypt, however, was very much on his mind. In 1852 he found time to write an important memorandum, a detailed proposal for the construction of a canal through the Isthmus of Suez. Naturally, he sent it on to Ruyssenaers in Cairo. But his friend felt that the idea would not appeal to the new viceroy, Abbas Pasha. Abbas was strongly influenced by the British, who were then, as they were later, violently opposed to the construction of a canal. There the matter ended. Unexpectedly, another tragic blow fell upon de Lesseps. His wife died of scarlet fever in 1853.

In the late summer of 1854, alone and cut off from the world, de Lesseps had reached his lowest point. He could not have known that his great moment was almost upon him. He could not have known that his great adventure was about to begin. And all because once he had been kind to a fat little boy in Cairo who hated exercise and loved to eat spaghetti.

45

III   JOURNEY TO EGYPT

It did not seem like the time or the place for great events to begin that quiet September morning in the French region of Berry. The year was 1854, and Monsieur de Lesseps, the retired diplomat, was hard at work in his new role as gentleman farmer and estate manager. In fact, at that very moment he was on top of a ladder supervising the addition of a story to a manor house.

In the courtyard below, the postman had just arrived with the morning mail from Paris. Workmen passed it up to de Lesseps. He sorted through the letters and then glanced at the morning paper. All of a sudden his attention was caught by a headline.

"I learned," said de Lesseps, describing the scene some

From batteries atop the Citadel, Egyptian soldiers have a panoramic view of Cairo, including the Mosque of Sultan Hassan. In the distance are the pyramids of Giza.

E. Brandard, sc.

time later, "that Abbas Pasha, Viceroy of Egypt, was dead. He was a very cruel and deceitful man and had succeeded Mohammed Ali and Ibrahim Pasha in the government of Egypt. His successor was the youngest son of Mohammed Ali, whom I had known well as a child, and taught to ride. He was enormously fat, and I made him exercise, much to the delight of his father."

De Lesseps at once climbed down from the top of the ladder. This was a marvelous piece of news. As he told his Dutch friend Ruyssenaers in a letter a few days later, he had lost no time in writing to the new viceroy, Mohammed Said, congratulating him on his accession. It was, he was sure, the most important letter he had ever written. Yet he could not help smiling at the curious turn of fate that had made fat little Prince Said the ruler of Egypt. De Lesseps thought of those days in Cairo twenty years ago, and he remembered Mohammed Ali's youngest son with amused affection.

As a boy of eleven, Prince Said had often slipped away from his guards and his tutors and had come sneaking into the French consulate. He was very fond of de Lesseps, who was teaching him how to ride and who seemed to be the only person who never treated him like a little boy. He used to come into the young consul's office and look at him with wide and pleading eyes. De Lesseps always understood.

Illustrated London News

Mohammed Said

Prince Said would speak very seriously in a low voice, and then de Lesseps would hurry him off to the kitchen. There the youngster would eat to his heart's content— spaghetti, which he loved, French pastry, and anything else he could find. All this feasting, of course, was very much against his father's orders. Mohammed Ali was disgusted with his overweight son and gave orders for a strict diet. He also set down a rigid schedule of exercise: two hours of climbing the masts of ships on the Nile, jumping rope, a run around the walls of Cairo twice a day, and horseback riding in the afternoons with the young French consul. This was harsh discipline for a boy of eleven, and it came close to killing the young Prince. Many people felt that Said had a glandular condition and was, quite literally, starving to death. It may well be that the extra food de Lesseps gave him saved his life. It was a strange friendship—between a Frenchman nearly thirty and an Egyptian prince of eleven—and one that neither of them ever forgot.

It was also a friendship that had the most unexpected consequences. For the day that Said came to sit on the throne of Egypt was the day that the story of the Suez

Canal began in earnest. Two widely different personalities had found their destinies—Said as ruler of Egypt and de Lesseps as builder of the Suez Canal. Power, at last, had become the ally of a dream.

It did not take Said long to answer the letter of congratulation. He too remembered the past with affection, and he invited his old friend to come to Egypt as soon as possible. De Lesseps read the Viceroy's letter with growing excitement. Only a short while ago he had thought that his career was over; now, at the age of forty-nine, he was making a new beginning.

Since his retirement from the diplomatic service in 1849, as he pointed out in his letter to Ruyssenaers, he had never stopped studying the question of the canal. At last he was ready to take action—and he was ready at the right moment.

De Lesseps realized that by 1854 the time had come when a canal through the Isthmus of Suez was practical and desirable. Twenty years before, when the idea of a canal had first captured his imagination, this had not been true. But now the world had changed dramatically. By the mid nineteenth century the great Industrial Revolution had swept through Europe, and in its wake had come a new prosperity and an enormous social and economic change. The old aristocracy was losing its hold, and wealth was pouring into the hands of a new middle class. Innumerable products and manufactured goods were wanted on a mass scale unknown in the past. The factories of England and the Continent needed raw materials from the Orient. They needed copra, jute, ore, and cotton.

These were requirements far different from the luxuries —furs, silks, and precious stones—that had once come through the canal of the pharaohs and later overland with the desert caravans. By the 1850's trade with the Far East was no longer a luxury; it had become essential to Europe's economic expansion. Iron ore was certainly too heavy to carry on camel back, and the way around the Cape of Good Hope took the better part of four months. A canal through the Isthmus of Suez would cut almost 5,800 miles from the Bombay to Marseilles run. The industrial countries of Europe, particularly England, needed more and more raw materials—and needed them faster and faster.

But de Lesseps knew that bringing materials to Europe faster along a canal's shorter route was only a part of the answer. There also had to be a way to carry all this tonnage across thousands of miles of water. A great revolution in maritime history was also taking place—the transition

The desirability of de Lesseps' idea for building a Suez canal is illustrated in the map above. A trip via the Isthmus of Suez would shorten the customary route from Marseilles to Bombay around the Cape of Good Hope by 5,800 miles.

In the desert outside Cairo, nineteenth-century travelers rest beside the great sphinx of Pharaoh Chephren at Giza. Visible in the background is Chephren's pyramid.

from sail to steam and from wooden ships to iron ones. This revolution was based on the development of the screw propeller, the use of iron for hulls, and the invention of the compound engine in 1854. Steamships in increasing numbers were in service. As early as 1824 a French naval vessel had steamed from Brest to French Guiana, and in 1832 the Royal Navy had sent a steamship from Plymouth to Barbados. A steamship fleet was incorporated in 1840 as the Cunard Line; by 1853 the Peninsular & Oriental line had an iron-screw steamer of over three thousand tons.

Now there were ships available with the speed and capacity to transport more of the riches of the Orient. The question of the most direct route to the Far East was the important one. At this very moment in history de Lesseps was about to present a complete plan for a canal through the Isthmus of Suez. He thought that the canal had become inevitable. His part in it, however, was not at all inevitable.

Others could have developed the Suez Canal as easily. But when he wrote to the new ruler of Egypt in 1854, he was trying to assure himself a role in that development.

In the early morning of November 7, 1854, Ferdinand de Lesseps began the practical phase of his great adventure. More than twenty years had gone by since the beginning of his dream—since the day in the hospital when he had first read Lepère's report. His ship was docking at Alexandria again, and in his pocket was his memorandum of 1852 on a Suez canal. The Egyptian sun shone down and sparkled on the green waters of Alexandria's harbor, and on this clear and beautiful day de Lesseps was full of the confidence that was never to leave him through all the days of the fifteen years that lay ahead.

When the ship docked, a member of Said's staff was there in a royal carriage to greet him. "I proceeded," he wrote later in the day to his mother-in-law, "to one of His Highness' villas, about two and a half miles from Alexandria on the Mahmudiya Canal. A whole battalion of servants was drawn up on the flight of stone steps, and they saluted me three times, putting out their right hands to the ground and then carrying them up to their foreheads." His old friend Said had put an entire palace at his disposal!

Before long, another member of the royal staff came and told de Lesseps that the Viceroy would see him at noon in the Gabbari Palace. De Lesseps dressed with care, putting on all his decorations, including the Legion of Honor he had received for his work in Cairo during the cholera epidemic of 1835. Then he was taken to a palace that stood on a promontory of the eastern harbor. Said received him with affection, and they talked at length about old times. Nothing was said of a Suez canal.

At the age of thirty-two Said's position in life was considerably different from what it had been the last time de Lesseps had seen him. Now there was no one to tell him what to do, or what not to do. Since the death of Abbas Pasha in July, he had become absolute ruler of Egypt. He answered to no one but the sultan of Turkey, at Constantinople. The sultan ruled over the Ottoman Empire, and Egypt was still a part of that empire. But Egyptian ties to Constantinople were loose; the sultan required little more than a show of obedience from the viceroy of Egypt—and substantial tribute.

Obviously, Said was now in a position to satisfy his every whim. And his whims were many. He was a giant of a man, with a red face and a full beard, who approached life

Passenger steamships move along the Mahmudiya Canal, a link between Cairo and Alexandria.

51

A seventeen-foot silver candelabra made in England for the prodigal Said dwarfs the onlookers below it.

with gusto and a certain amount of genial vulgarity. His mood alternated between moments of violent rage and uncontrolled generosity. Practical jokes were a passion with him, and he went to great lengths to amuse himself. On one occasion he shocked his ministers by walking through loose gunpowder while holding a lighted candle in each hand and then demanded that they follow his example—simply to see how strong their nerves were. His character was a paradox: a mixture of Oriental capriciousness and European culture. He had been educated in France and was fond of all things French. But he loved ostentation, extravagance, and splendor. Above all, he loved uniforms. There was nothing he would rather do than play at being a soldier.

In fact, he told de Lesseps, he was just about to lead a march across the Western Desert to Cairo. Ten thousand troops were going on maneuvers, and he thought it would be a good idea if his old friend came along. De Lesseps jumped at the chance to spend time alone with Said.

A few days later a splendid procession passed through the gates of Alexandria and turned toward the desert. De Lesseps rode at the right hand of the Viceroy—an unusual place of honor for a foreigner. Bedouin scouts galloped into the desert ahead of the column. Brightly colored banners unfurled in the soft wind that came across the sands. Following Said and his generals was a squadron of lancers wearing breastplates and ancient Saracen helmets. Then came artillery and Egyptian footsoldiers and, finally, camels carrying necessities for the royal party. There were tents and rugs, china from France, ice, water, and fresh provisions. It was a strange military expedition.

That night, having passed beyond the ancient baths of Cleopatra, the column pitched camp in the desert. De Lesseps made up his mind to approach Said the next day on the matter of the Suez Canal. There was no point in further delay. The unpredictable Viceroy was enjoying the expedition enormously and seemed to be in one of his good moods. Surely the proper moment had come.

On the following morning de Lesseps was awake before dawn. It was November 15, 1854, and he would remember the exact date for the rest of his life. He left his tent at once. Standing in the sand and wrapped in a red dressing gown, he felt (he said later) like some exotic sheik from Mecca. The first light of the sun was beginning to outline the horizon, yet the day promised to be overcast. Suddenly something incredible happened. There appeared in the west, he wrote that night in his journal, "where the sky is cloudy, a very brilliant rainbow, running from east to west.''

The rainbow was exactly what de Lesseps needed to convince himself that this would be the luckiest day of his life. There was no question of failure now. In the first moments of this new day he was certain that Said would give permission for a canal to be built. Had there not been a miraculous omen in the sky?

He dressed quickly and spent the day putting together his notes on the canal and otherwise preparing for the attack on Said. At five o'clock he mounted his Arab pony and galloped through camp toward the Viceroy's tent. In front of the royal tent a high barrier had been erected. De Lesseps, always an excellent horseman, cleared it with ease. The Viceroy saw him, and so did his generals. They cheered and applauded, for horsemanship is considered a great art by the Arabs. De Lesseps dismounted and went into the Viceroy's tent. His head was high and his heart was full of confidence.

Said was waiting, and he motioned him to sit down. They were alone, sitting side by side on a divan. Through the opening of the tent de Lesseps could see that the sun was beginning to go down. But he remembered that morn-

The Viceroy's soldiers stand at attention during inspection on the parade grounds of the Alexandria garrison. The troops wear white cotton uniforms and carry muskets.

BOTH: *Illustrated London News*

53

ing's rainbow. Taking a deep breath, he turned to Said and began to outline his plan for a canal through the Isthmus of Suez. De Lesseps had a moment of nervousness, for he had not lost sight of the fact that the idea had been opposed by Said's father, Mohammed Ali.

Nevertheless, the Frenchman went on to explain the need the world had for such a highway to the Far East. He emphasized the honor and importance the canal would bring to Egypt. He went into the history of the ancient canal and appealed to Said's vanity by implying that the construction of a new canal would be a feat greater than anything the pharaohs had accomplished. Yet he was vague about the details of cost and construction. He did, however, dwell at length on how the canal was bound to bring the nations of the world closer together. In this he was very close to the philosophy of Prosper Enfantin.

"Isn't it obvious," he told Said, "that this great work will arouse universal enthusiasm and be greeted by the active . . . participation of men of vision in all countries?"

The Viceroy listened carefully. Then he asked a few questions and settled back in silence on the divan. Perhaps he was considering his role as a man of vision and patron of a great project. At last he turned to de Lesseps.

"I am convinced," he said. "I accept your plan. We will concern ourselves during the rest of our expedition as to the means of carrying it out. You may regard the matter as settled, and trust to me."

Then he clapped his hands and called for his generals. He told them briefly of the new plans for a Suez canal. They were quick to applaud the idea—perhaps because it was unwise to contradict the Viceroy or perhaps because de Lesseps had just gained their respect by his daring horsemanship. Probably the generals did not care one way

Egyptian peasants draw water from the Nile with shadufs. This system, used since ancient times, is based on a simple principle: a bucket swinging from a weighted pole.

or another. But Said seemed pleased, and he called for dinner. They all sat on pillows on the ground, and a huge silver tureen was brought in. Together they dipped their spoons into the soup. And de Lesseps could not help thinking that this was a fitting symbol of the great harmony that had just been achieved. In his journal he wrote that this dinner ended "the most important negotiation I ever undertook, or am likely to undertake."

After dinner de Lesseps gave Mohammed Said a copy of his 1852 memorandum on a Suez canal. It was actually material he had paraphrased in their earlier conversation. (In the months to come, some of the Egyptian ministers would go so far as to say that Said had never read it at all. But that would not bother de Lesseps; the decision had already been made.) He returned to his tent, overwhelmed by the knowledge that his dream of twenty years was beginning to take form at last.

It was incredible to think that he had been in Egypt for only eight days. It was incredible to think with what ease he had persuaded Said to undertake so vast a scheme as the cutting of a canal through the Isthmus of Suez. Only the strength of an old friendship and the force of de Lesseps' great charm and sincerity could have accomplished it.

On the following morning the expedition continued across the Western Desert. But by the time they reached the Nile at Neguileh, the changeable Said had lost his enthusiasm for the routine of army maneuvers. He transferred the royal party to several yachts, which were riding at anchor in the Nile. Said's own yacht, *Mahroussa*, was unbelievably luxurious; she had been built in England for the late Abbas Pasha at a cost of $500,000. Among her many sumptuous features were fittings of solid silver, costly paintings, divans covered with cloth of gold, and a dining room forty feet long. In such comfort the royal party moved along the great river toward Cairo.

During the journey de Lesseps and Said worked out details for the preliminary organization of a Suez canal company. These details were the basis of what came to be known as the First Concession, given later under the official date of November 30, 1854. It was drafted by Said (or so he later insisted) and gave his permission for the creation of a Suez canal company. The first director, Said indicated, was to be Ferdinand de Lesseps, "my devoted friend of high rank and exalted birth."

Among the various articles of concession the most important were these: the director was to be chosen by the

Egyptian government; the concession was to be in effect for ninety-nine years from the date of opening; and all the necessary land on the isthmus was to be given to the company by the Viceroy himself. The canal was to be open to the ships of all nations. And any future profits from it were to be divided as follows: 15 per cent to the Egyptian government, 75 per cent to the company, and 10 per cent to the founders, those original investors who were to give de Lesseps his first working capital. Later a final clause, which did not seem particularly important at the time, was attached to the concession. It cautioned that the construction of the canal could not begin without permission from Egypt's actual ruler, the sultan of Turkey.

So the details were arranged, and finally the royal flotilla reached Cairo. Within a few days—on November 25, 1854—Said called a meeting of all the representatives of foreign governments in Egypt. He was anxious to announce his great plan for a Suez canal. Naturally de Lesseps was asked to attend.

In the great hall of the Citadel, from the throne that had once been used by his father, Mohammed Ali, the Viceroy received the foreign consuls. Among others, the French consul general was there and also Ruyssenaers of Holland and Mr. Frederick Bruce, who represented Great Britain.

Said announced that he had decided to cut a canal through the Isthmus of Suez and that he had permitted a company to be organized with Ferdinand de Lesseps as its

Said entertains forty-eight guests in the lavish dining salon on his yacht Faid Gihaad. *Liveried servants carrying delicacies to the diners move over carpeted floors.*

Faid Gihaad, *one of many luxury ships owned by Said, was built in 1852. As an incidental embellishment, the vessel could carry 418 guns. Seven gun ports are visible on either side of her paddle wheel.*

Illustrated London News

director. He outlined the most important terms of the First Concession. Then he turned to de Lesseps.

"This is what we intend to do," he said. "Is it not?"

De Lesseps nodded and spoke briefly, being careful to emphasize the fact that inspiration for the project had come from Said. The various foreign representatives were surprised at this piece of news, but they applauded politely. De Lesseps was quick to notice, however, that Mr. Bruce did not applaud at all. In fact, he seemed nervous and ill at ease. It was a first hint of trouble to come.

De Lesseps knew that he would have to have the British on his side. Within forty-eight hours he had written a personal letter to Bruce. It was a masterpiece of enthusiasm and, unfortunately, innocence as well. He saw fit to put all of his cards on the table. He tried to point out the many benefits Great Britain would derive from a Suez canal.

"Anything which contributes to the extension of trade, industry, and navigation," he wrote, "must be specially advantageous to England, considering that she takes rank before all other powers in the importance of her navy, her manufacturing products, and her commercial relations. Only the unfortunate prejudices, which, owing to political differences, have so long divided France and England could have accredited the belief that the opening of a Suez canal, a work of civilization and progress, would be detrimental to British interests."

De Lesseps was logical, and he was persuasive. Certainly it was clever of him to have approached the representative of Great Britain on a personal level. Yet it was naïve of him to have supposed that the matter would end there. In Bruce's lack of enthusiasm at the Citadel he should have read the obstinacy of his first, and his greatest, enemy—the British Empire.

INDIA TO ENGLAND
BEFORE THE CANAL

Before the Suez Canal was built, the long voyage from India to London took a strong constitution and hearty spirits. Voyagers crossing the Indian Ocean (left)—the first lap of the trip—relieve the tedium of endless hours aboard ship by reading or playing a ring-toss game. Despite the extreme heat and the crowded quarters, passengers maintain their decorum, encasing themselves in the layers of clothing considered proper for such a voyage. One traveler described the day's final ritual: "We soon turn in regardless of scorpions and other visitors and sleep until the steward wakes us with a cup of tea at six." Aden, a coaling station en route, was a welcome landmark for travelers (bottom left). Here, passengers could disembark and do a bit of sightseeing: "In the morning we rowed ashore; mounted a donkey to see the sights; rode up wonderful rocks—breakneck places, but fearlessly, on our sure-footed donkeys. We turned a corner when all at once Aden . . . burst upon our view." The voyage then continued across the Red Sea, and travelers got off at or near Suez for the overland trip to Cairo. By 1858, railroad tracks reached to Suez (below), and this convenience re-

(continued on the following page)

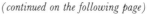

lieved travelers of the tiring carriage ride across the isthmus. For the adventurous, however, the furious pace by van (right) was full of excitement. An earlier passenger described the uncomfortable but eventful ride: "Five vans . . . started in a set—changed horses at post houses at stages of about six to seven miles . . . Accomplished the journey in some seventeen or eighteen hours." As a postscript, the writer wistfully added, "Soon the rail will be opened all the way to Suez; and the enterprising traveler will be able to sleep as soundly across the desert as he would from London to Brighton." After considerable bumping and tossing, and a stopover at Cairo, the weary traveler arrived in Alexandria. Below, mail, camels, and passengers arrive at the door of Alexandria's post office. At last, after crossing the Mediterranean, came the welcome sight of the English coast from the Channel. The mail from India (opposite, below) comes in at Folkestone.

ALL: *Illustrated London News*

IV OPPOSITION FROM

In 1855 Sir Stratford Canning, Viscount Stratford de Redcliffe, was Queen Victoria's ambassador to Constantinople, a position he had held for more than a dozen years. Somehow he had managed to intimidate the whole of the Ottoman Empire, and throughout the Middle East he was known as Sultan Stratford, the Terrible Englishman. Through years of hard work, he had created an impressive image for himself and had become a symbol of the pride and stubbornness of the British Empire.

Constantinople was a unique and important capital. It was the heart of the Ottoman Empire and the center of all the complex politics of the Middle East. The sultan of Turkey was its ruler, and the grand vizier was his prime minister. Beautifully situated on the Golden Horn, Constantinople was an Oriental city of minarets, harems, and fantastic palaces. Political intrigue and espionage formed the pattern of its daily life. People from all over the Middle East swarmed through the city, searching for influence and position. Foreign ambassadors practiced the dangerous game of power politics. In fact, at the moment, Great Britain, France, and Turkey were drawn up against Russia in the Crimean War (1854–56). Constantinople was the key to the Middle East, and the city was the scene of a constant struggle for power.

And the greatest power there seemed to be in the hands of Lord Stratford de Redcliffe. Tall, with an imposing presence and an imperious manner, he moved haughtily through the intrigues of the Ottoman court—here exerting his influence and there destroying an opponent. In his own way he was as much of a despot as the sultan himself. The grand vizier, Reshid Pasha, was largely under

The sultan of Turkey pays a call at the British embassy in Constantinople, a reversal of diplomatic protocol and an unprecedented compliment to the British. Customarily, the sultan held audience only in his own palace.

THE BRITISH

Illustrated London News

his influence, and Sir Stratford effectively called the tune in the Middle East. The tune was usually a British one.

In February of 1855, Ferdinand de Lesseps arrived in the Ottoman capital determined to obtain the sultan's permission to dig a canal. De Lesseps regarded the permission as a formality; he did not foresee any extraordinary problems. He was full of confidence, and at this point in his journey, full of innocent optimism as well. This was understandable, for his conquest of Mohammed Said had been a spectacularly easy one. However, he had made no allowance for Sir Stratford, who stood, with folded arms, blocking the way to Suez.

Moreover, the British government supported his opposition by sending him direct and explicit instructions: "Her Majesty's Government considers that the canal would be useless even if it were possible to execute it, and the concession desired by M. de Lesseps is highly objectionable for political reasons."

What, exactly, were these "political reasons?" Certainly they should have come as no surprise to de Lesseps. After twenty-five years in the diplomatic service he was more than familiar with them. It was simply that he had underestimated their importance in the present situation.

At different times in the course of history, Great Britain and France had been both desperate enemies and uneasy allies. True, the Napoleonic Wars had ended on the field of Waterloo in 1815, and the two countries were fighting now on the same side in the Crimea. Yet, even after forty years, suspicion of France was still active in England. And it had been particularly active since 1852, when Napoleon III had established the Second Empire in France. Memories of his uncle, the first Napoleon, were not easy to erase. British government officials still remembered that Bonaparte had invaded Egypt with the particular purpose of extending French influence to the Far East. Britain was extremely sensitive about the Mediterranean and her empire in India. The seas must remain open to her merchant marine.

Lord Stratford de Redcliffe

Britain's powerful navy patrolled the waters from Gibraltar to Alexandria and guarded the sea lanes that led to India around the Cape of Good Hope. Any threat in these two areas was a blow at her heart. And it happened in 1855 that the Frenchman Ferdinand de Lesseps was making such a threat. To Great Britain the idea of a canal through the Isthmus of Suez was unthinkable. She had long dominated the route to the Far East around the Cape of Good Hope and was not interested in any change. Moreover, the

The sultan, seated beneath a canopy, is rowed across the Bosporus in his state barge. The ruler's sword bearer sits in front of the huge peacock that decorates the prow. The other vessel, equally ornate, carries the sultan's ministers.

canal now proposed—the British government felt with some justice—would be monopolized by the French, despite de Lesseps' insistence that it was to be an international undertaking. If France controlled the canal, British prestige would decline throughout the Middle East. Her Indian empire would be in danger and so, too, would her leadership in trade with the Orient. In the eyes of the British government, the political aspect of a Suez canal was a simple one. De Lesseps had hold of a dangerous idea, and to add to the unpleasantness, he was a Frenchman as well. The British were going to fight, and the first battlefield they chose was Constantinople.

When the attack began in the first months of 1855, de Lesseps found himself facing the enemy entirely alone. It was a situation in which he was to find himself often during the next fifteen years. In Constantinople he was no longer on the familiar ground of Egypt. Said was far away, and distance considerably diminished his powers as an ally. And Sir Stratford had seen to it that every possible obstacle was put in his way. The sultan could not be approached except through his grand vizier, and Reshid Pasha was under Sir Stratford's thumb. For a time de Lesseps struggled. But soon he saw how cleverly a silken net of

65

intrigue had been slipped over his head. Finally he had had enough. He forgot his diplomatic training, and with uncharacteristic bluntness, made a direct appeal to the British ambassador.

He made it at a dinner given by the Turkish minister of foreign affairs one February night in 1855. The conversation was general and of no consequence until de Lesseps turned it to the subject of the canal. Once more he outlined the advantages it would offer the world in general—and Britain in particular. "Sultan Stratford" listened politely. Then he spoke with icy exactness.

"All that you say is quite sound," he told de Lesseps. "But it is not to be thought of for a hundred years to come. It is inopportune."

And that was the end of the matter. In the days to come, de Lesseps sent letters to Sir Stratford; they went unanswered. He requested interviews; they were smoothly postponed. Meanwhile, de Lesseps tried to convince the Ottoman ministers that the real opposition to the canal came not from the British government but from the ambassador himself. Nothing did any good, and he soon found himself at the end of a blind alley. One day he was told that his request for the sultan's permission had been set aside for the moment. It had disappeared into a dark void where endless delays could indeed keep it for a hundred years to come.

A tarboosh decorated with an emblem and feathers crowns the head of the Grand Vizier Reshid Pasha.

But it was not in de Lesseps' nature to surrender—not after twenty years of dreaming and planning. His attack would simply have to take another direction. Victory was not to be found among the charades and intrigues of Constantinople. It was to be found in England.

On the trip back to Europe de Lesseps examined his position with cool detachment. In those weeks after Said had granted him the First Concession, he had been foolishly optimistic. For the concession was, after all, no more than a scrap of paper. In some ways the prospect of a Suez canal was just as remote as it had been back in Alexandria in 1832. Yet de Lesseps had taken one giant step. He knew his enemies, and he had looked them in the face.

Although England was of course the principal enemy, there were others. There was money, for instance—or rather the lack of it. And there was a third enemy he had not even considered to any great extent. It was the hostile desert that separated the Mediterranean from the Red Sea and waited silently on the Isthmus of Suez. Perhaps any one of these three obstacles would have stopped a less determined man. But de Lesseps was not about to betray his dream. Not for the stubborn English or for a lack of money or for the sand barrier at Suez.

It was not impossible to overcome these enemies, for in what had clearly become a war, there were some important advantages on de Lesseps' side. First, there was the unshakable friendship of Said with all the resources of Egypt behind him. And, through another fortunate circumstance, de Lesseps could expect some help from the French government. In 1853 his cousin Eugénie de Montijo had married Napoleon III and was now Empress of the French. She could certainly be a powerful ally in his struggle. But there was something in his favor even more important than the friendship of these two rulers. De Lesseps sensed correctly that the trend of the future was on his side.

The nineteenth century was an age of change and progress. In every country, people were fascinated with machinery and technology. Only a few years before, in England's Great Exhibition of 1851 at the Crystal Palace, the technical aspects of a new civilization had been fully revealed for the first time. An engineering feat such as a Suez canal would have great appeal in an age of bridges, steamships, and railroads. Trade and communication had become bywords. Nowhere was this more true than in England.

And it was to England that de Lesseps now carried his attack. There was little to be gained by fencing with Lord Stratford de Redcliffe in the unreal Arabian Nights' atmosphere of Constantinople.

Industrialized Britain presented scenes such as factory smokestacks nearly obscuring the view of St. Paul's in London (above) and a huge bridge being built in Wales.

W. G. READER, *Life in Victorian England*

De Lesseps looked up at the white cliffs of Dover on a June morning in 1855. England was an island fortress, and he had come to conquer it. He relished the prospect of the battle before him, for he was a man who grew stronger in the face of conflict and challenge. As one biographer put it, he had "the energy of a dynamo, the driving power of a sledge hammer, and the magnetism of a lodestar." And he would need these qualities in his personal war on England.

To some extent de Lesseps had laid the groundwork for his attack. He had written a number of letters—to newspapers, politicians, and important businessmen. In each he had struck a similar chord, emphasizing that a Suez canal would benefit the world by breaking down "the barriers which still divide men, races, and nations." He also pointed out, over and over again, the financial profit it would bring to England. One letter in particular contained all the essential propaganda he was to direct against England. It had been written to Richard Cobden, a prominent politician and economist and a leading advocate of free trade. De Lesseps had written to Cobden only a few weeks after the First Concession had been granted by Said.

"Some persons assert," de Lesseps wrote, "that the project will excite hostility in England. I cannot believe it. Your statesmen are too enlightened for me to admit such an idea. What! England has herself one half of the general trade with the Indies and China; she possesses an immense empire in Asia; she can reduce by a third the costs of her trade and reduce by one half the distance. . . . If by any possible chance the difficulties with which we are already threatened should arise, I hope that the public spirit which is so powerful in England will soon override interested opposition and antiquated objections."

It was de Lesseps' misfortune, soon after his arrival in England, to come face to face with the leader of the antiquated opposition—Henry John Temple, Viscount Palmerston, Prime Minister of Great Britain.

In 1855 Lord Palmerston was a crusty old man of seventy-one. He still was, as he had always been, tactless and opinionated and the very image of a tenacious John Bull. Through the self-confidence and obstinacy born of a long and successful career in politics he had turned himself into something of an idol to mid-Victorian England. Even Queen Victoria had her difficulties with him. "He had many valuable qualities," she once remarked, "though many bad ones, and we had, God knows, terrible trouble with him about foreign affairs."

Unhappily, de Lesseps and the canal were solidly in the area of foreign affairs. Years before, Palmerston had been foreign secretary, and even as prime minister, foreign affairs was a field in which he constantly interfered. Like many another politician in nineteenth-century England, he was violently antagonistic to the French and suspicious of their motives.

So he could not have been overjoyed when de Lesseps appeared one morning at No. 10 Downing Street, armed with a letter of introduction. Palmerston received the Frenchman cordially enough, though de Lesseps saw that he had the look of a man whose mind was already made up. For once, Palmerston was reasonably polite. But he made his position on the matter of a Suez canal more than clear.

"I will not hesitate to tell you," he said, "what my apprehensions are. They consist in the first place of the fear of seeing the commercial and maritime relations of Great Britain upset by the opening of a new route which, in being

Muttonchop sideburns and an iras-
cible expression distinguish the
face of Prime Minister Palmerston.

open to the navigation of all nations, will deprive us of the advantages which we at present possess."

De Lesseps listened to the familiar refrain and saw the stubbornness in the old man's face. Yet, for the most part, everything was said in the most jovial of spirits. De Lesseps remembered that Palmerston ushered him out of the office with an "air of bonhomie."

Palmerston, however, was not nearly so polite when he came to discuss the subject in the House of Commons. One day a member asked him to explain why he was so violently opposed to the idea of a canal through the Isthmus of Suez.

"The most charitable view which I can take of the scheme," thundered Palmerston, "the most innocent light in which it can be regarded is, in my opinion, that it is the greatest bubble [financial swindle] which was ever imposed

MORAINE 1855

upon the credulity and simplicity of the people of this country."

He admitted to Commons that every pressure had been exerted at Constantinople by the British government to prevent the scheme from being carried out. He did acknowledge, however, that Monsieur de Lesseps was a "very persevering gentleman." He also hinted that he was little more than a swindler. He painted a black picture of England's future, should the canal be built. Egypt would surely revolt from the Ottoman Empire and so fall under the domination of France. The Mediterranean would soon become a French lake. There would be French cruisers patrolling the canal and the Red Sea. The threat to British India was obvious.

During his visits to England over the course of the next three years, de Lesseps saw Palmerston on other occasions. The substance of the Prime Minister's conversation was always the same. The canal was "physically impracticable" to build, since it would soon fill up with sand, and, even if it were possible, no financial profit could be expected from it. Of course, de Lesseps knew that the motive underlying these objections was fear of the French. Palmerston was so often violent on the subject that de Lesseps began to wonder whether he was dealing with a statesman or a madman. He soon came to the conclusion that, like the obstinate Stratford de Redcliffe, Lord Palmerston would simply have to be bypassed. The war would have to be won in some other way.

De Lesseps believed in the intelligence and rationality of the average man. So he carried the diplomatic battle— as he was to carry the financial one—directly to the people. He counted on the strength of that English "public spirit" he had mentioned to Cobden. In 1855, in London and Paris, he published a pamphlet that contained the most persuasive of his arguments. It was called *The Isthmus of Suez Question*, and it left no doubt as to the desirability of the canal. The pamphlet was widely read, and de Lesseps came to be regarded as something of a celebrity.

In the first week of May, 1856, he managed to be presented to Queen Victoria herself. At the same time he had a

THOMAS WRIGHT, *The History of France*

The political rivalry between France and England did not prevent their monarchs from exchanging visits in 1855. Above, Queen Victoria invests Napoleon III with the Order of the Garter during his visit to London in May. Opposite, the Queen reviews a military parade in Paris in August.

Even in an era of structural innovation, London's Crystal Palace was an engineering marvel of iron and glass. The domed, two-storied hall, built to house the Great Exhibition of 1851, was 1,800 feet long. Manufacturers from around the world displayed goods ranging from heavy machinery to handcrafts. In this contemporary illustration, Victorian strollers look over the 1,500 exhibits, including display cases with such arresting items as "philosophical instruments" (left). National flags hang from the gallery over the crowded central aisle.

A band of mutinous Sepoys divide the booty captured in an attack on a British garrison while other native troops assault the defenders.

long conversation with her husband, Prince Albert. The Prince had been the patron of the Great Exhibition of 1851 and was enthusiastic about every form of technical progress. De Lesseps was excited by Prince Albert's interest in the Suez project, and he wrote to his cousin the Empress Eugénie about it.

During the years from 1855 to 1858, he kept in constant touch with France, crossing back and forth between London and Paris. Through Eugénie he was trying to persuade Napoleon III to give official support to a Suez canal. He hoped the Emperor would be influenced by the fact that Prince Albert was "well disposed" toward it. Napoleon III was interested to learn that de Lesseps' campaign in England was beginning to have results, but Napoleon did not want trouble with England, and he remained undecided.

As the final stage of that campaign, de Lesseps arranged a series of trips to leading industrial centers. Accompanied by Sir Daniel Lange, his English representative, and a trunkful of maps and plans and reports, de Lesseps invaded the north of England. The tour was an exhausting one. He spoke in town meetings in Manchester and Liverpool. He went to Edinburgh and as far north as Aberdeen and even to Belfast and Dublin. He talked to the owners of shipyards, mines, and factories. He spoke to bankers, merchants, and directors of steamship companies. He talked to those who traded with the Far East. He called on editors at *The Times* in London and at other newspaper offices. Soon he had covered Britain with a blanket of propaganda.

Nor was he wrong about the strength of the English "public spirit." The people as a whole were in favor of his idea, and businessmen clearly saw the advantages of a new and faster route to the Orient. They saw these advantages in terms of pounds and shillings. Yet no one cared to lend him money, and there were still many voices against him. Some said that the canal would simply be a stagnant ditch; others predicted it would be filled by the sand of the desert.

Sensible Englishmen, however, were on his side. Only the government remained adamant. Only the government prevented him from getting the sultan's permission to go ahead. Lord Palmerston was still on the scene, a jaunty old villain with fixed ideas.

But a day came when the opposition to the canal received a serious setback. In March, 1857, near Calcutta, the disastrous Great Mutiny began. Native troops revolted against the British, and reinforcements had to be rushed to India in order to put down the rebellion. Of course, the only way they could be rushed from England was by ship on the four-month-long voyage around the Cape of Good Hope. It was painfully obvious that a canal through the Isthmus of Suez would have saved countless British lives. As it turned out, the British government was finally forced to beg Said's permission to send troops through Egypt overland across the isthmus to the Gulf of Suez. English newspapers were quick to see their government's folly. "Nothing could be a more complete avowal of the utility of M. de Lesseps' scheme," said the London *Daily News*, "and the action of the Government is the implicit condemnation of Lord Palmerston and Lord Stratford de Redcliffe."

A personal opponent of de Lesseps' was removed when, because of a general lack of confidence in his government, Lord Palmerston's cabinet fell in February, 1858.

A Royal Artillery advance guard, en route to India, directs the unloading of supplies at Alexandria.

THE PARIS OF NAPOLEON III

The most lasting and perhaps the most controversial venture undertaken by Napoleon III (below) was the transformation of the narrow streets and squalid quarters of Paris into the wide boulevards and elegant buildings for which the French capital is known today. This nineteenth-century urban renewal was carried out by Napoleon's chief city planner, Baron Haussmann. During the rebuilding, sections of Paris resembled disaster areas. The panorama at bottom right includes a razed section that became a plaza in front of Notre Dame on the venerable Ile de la Cité. While Paris was having her face lifted, the uppercrust of the Second Empire continued its pleasure-seeking existence. At right, ladies in their voluminous crinolines and gentlemen in uniforms circulate through the marble halls of the Hôtel de Ville (city hall) during a grand ball.

77

Other, less backward-looking, politicians were about to enter upon the stage. W. E. Gladstone, a future prime minister, said in Parliament: "I am unwilling to set up the Indian Empire of Great Britain in opposition to the general interests of mankind, or to the general sentiment of Europe." He went on to calm English fears about a possible French domination of Egypt: "Is it not a canal which would necessarily fall within the control of the first maritime power of Europe? It is England, and no foreign country, which would obtain the command of it." His words were an accurate prophecy of the future.

At this stage in his war against England there were other developments that must have delighted de Lesseps. He had not spent all of his time in England. In addition to his trips to Paris, he had returned to Cairo to keep Said's enthusiasm alive. And he had continued to exert pressure at Constantinople. From these activities there had come some results. He had received a promise of support, even if somewhat vague, from the Empress Eugénie. On January 5, 1856, Said had granted him a second concession, which guaranteed further help from his government and provided for Egyptian laborers to dig the canal. And, in December, 1857, de Lesseps learned that Lord Stratford de Redcliffe's long career at Constantinople had come to an end. Early in 1858, Reshid Pasha, the devious grand vizier, died. Now it would no longer be so difficult to approach the sultan, and public opinion in England was beginning to resent British interference in Ottoman affairs.

But the favorable winds did not last for long. Within fifteen months the unconquerable Palmerston was back as prime minister, as powerful as before and every bit as opposed to the canal.

De Lesseps, however, had one important weapon that had not been his when he first arrived in England. He had a detailed engineering report denying Palmerston's theory that the canal was impossible to build. In the summer of 1855, de Lesseps had formed a group called the International Scientific Commission, and in December, he led them into the desert from Suez. Linant Bey, his old friend from the early days in Egypt, joined him in the survey. The engineers presented their report in the first month of 1856. It was an extremely favorable one, and everything

In the formal portrait opposite, Ferdinand de Lesseps displays the ribbon and badge of the Legion of Honor, awarded for his services as a diplomat.

79

seemed to point to the technical success of the canal.

The engineers reaffirmed the 1846 survey that had proved there was no significant difference in water level between the Mediterranean and the Red Sea. They felt adequate harbors could be built at both ends of the isthmus. In fact, there was a reasonably good harbor already at Suez. They pointed out that there was very little rock to blast along the hundred miles of desert and that there was hardly any chance of the canal filling with sand. All in all, the engineering problem seemed to be a relatively simple one. They estimated that the whole project would cost in the neighborhood of two hundred million francs—a figure representing eight million pounds, or forty million dollars.

Armed with this favorable report, de Lesseps felt that nothing could stop him. Yet few of the leading bankers in England, or in Europe, had been enthusiastic, and the politicians were still opposed. At last de Lesseps decided on a characteristically bold move. He remembered what Prince Metternich had told him during one of his recent trips to the Continent. The clever old diplomat pointed out that once the canal was built, there would be no opposition to it. He urged de Lesseps to move ahead with his plans

Britain's policy regarding a Suez canal was forced on Sultan Abdul Medjid (right). The French view of his opposition is shown in the cartoon above. An old Turk obstructs passage of a train on which the word "civilization" is written.

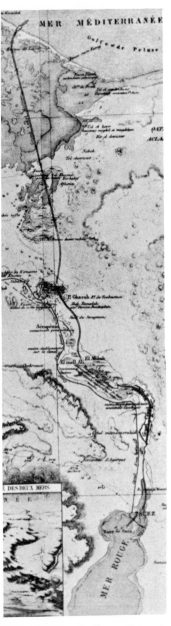

despite Palmerston and the delays at Constantinople. Money was the only problem to take seriously.

This was the kind of advice de Lesseps had been waiting to hear. He was tired of endless diplomatic intrigue. In spite of his training in the French foreign service, he was essentially a direct man—a man of action. He saw now that only audacity could win the battle. Only audacity could build the canal against so much opposition. Although the odds were against him, he would go on alone—attacking again and striking unexpectedly from another direction. For the moment he would forget about England. He would concentrate on France.

Lord Palmerston could go to the devil and so could the sultan of Turkey, along with all the cautious bankers and nervous diplomats. Whether they liked it or not, the canal was going forward. There would be no more delays. De Lesseps remembered what Said's father, Mohammed Ali, had told him many years ago: "Always keep this in mind, my young friend, when you have any important scheme on hand, depend on yourself alone."

Late in the summer of 1858, de Lesseps returned to France to begin the final round of his struggle.

The map above indicates the route from the Red Sea to the Mediterranean suggested by Linant Bey and Mougel Bey in their study for the International Scientific Commission. The town of Suez (right) would be the Red Sea entry port.

The British and the French move their cannon into position at the siege of Sebastopol in 1855. Although the two pow

ared the glory of winning the Crimean War, the British government continued to oppose a French-built Suez canal.

V

FINANCING THE CANAL

Baron James Rothschild was amused. His visitor on this late-summer morning in 1858 did not seem to have a clear grasp of financial matters. But de Lesseps had come to Paris to raise money. As he told Rothschild, he was interested in setting up a public subscription and selling shares of stock in a Suez canal company.

"If you wish," said the Baron, "I will open your subscription at my office."

De Lesseps considered the proposal. Certainly he needed 200,000,000 francs ($40,000,000). But he was suspicious of bankers, particularly since they had been so opposed to his project in the past. Finally he asked a question.

"And what will you charge me for it?"

"Good heavens!" said Rothschild with a smile, "it is plain you are not a man of business. It is always five percent."

De Lesseps thought for a moment. "Five per cent on two hundred million? Why, that makes ten million! I shall hire a place for twelve hundred francs and do my own business equally well."

And this is exactly what he did. The office he rented in Paris in the Place Vendôme was barely large enough for himself and his three assistants. But it was in keeping with the method that he had chosen to raise money in the early autumn of 1858. It was a simple method, and one that cut through all the complexities of international finance. He

Three Second Empire dandies stroll up the Rue de Castiglione toward the Place Vendôme in the heart of fashionable Paris. At the center of the square rises the column honoring Napoleon Bonaparte's 1805 Austerlitz victory.

had decided to operate alone, on what amounted to an amateur basis.

He was motivated by pride and stubbornness and more than a little desperation. Although he had shifted his attack from London to Paris, his position had remained unchanged. The Suez project was at a standstill. It was true that the Viceroy had given him the assurance of complete cooperation. But permission still had not come from the sultan at Constantinople. Great Britain, at least on an official level, continued to oppose the whole idea.

In addition, no financial help had come from France or any other European country despite his many propaganda trips around the Continent. Money simply was not available to him. It was an unhappy fact that most bankers, since the granting of the First Concession in 1854, had turned their backs on him. De Lesseps felt that he could not afford the commission of reputable bankers like Rothschild. "They are not reasonable," he complained.

However, Paris, during the time of the Second Empire, was full of speculators, shady financiers, and gamblers more than willing to slice into a pie worth two hundred million francs. Their motives, however, were not above

The chic Paris gathering place for the intelligentsia of the Second Empire was the Cafe Tortoni. Below, at sidewalk tables in front of the cafe, writers, statesmen, and diplomats sharpen their wits.

Baron James Rothschild, head of the French branch of the famous international banking family, was often deeply involved in the financial affairs of the Second Empire. By 1862, he was chief banker to Napoleon III.

suspicion, and de Lesseps was on guard in this financial underworld. As he said to his mother-in-law one day, "I am not tempted to turn over my affairs to birds of prey and wolves of high finance." And he told her that more than anything else he wanted to create the canal "without sordid motives and without greed of gold."

Under the circumstances, his decision to sell shares in a canal company himself was the only remaining alternative. But a great deal of work was necessary before any stock could be put on the market. For the moment, relying on money privately obtained from the founders (friends who were allowed to invest before the public sale of stock), he managed to keep his small office going. Certain steps had to be taken immediately. In the first place he had to increase the amount of publicity given to the newspapers about a Suez canal. It was essential to keep the public informed and the proposed canal constantly before its eyes. Otherwise, there was little chance of selling the stock at all. It was a demanding job, but de Lesseps was up to it.

He was tireless. All through the autumn of 1858 he worked at an incredible pace. Using the Place Vendôme office as headquarters, he carried on his battle. He wrote letter after letter and conducted countless interviews. He seized every possible opportunity to talk about the canal—arguing, persuading, pleading, and using all of his great charm. He stayed in constant touch with the Empress

Eugénie, and, through her, with Napoleon III. Finally, he was clever enough to obtain unofficial support from the French government by convincing Jérôme Napoleon to act as "protector" of the new company. This genial prince was first cousin to Napoleon III and a person of influence in the opulent world of the Second Empire. His patronage of the company was a triumph for de Lesseps and a feat that required all of his diplomacy to accomplish. Naturally, it would help convince the general public of the virtue of investing in a canal. It would also be a giant step toward persuading the Emperor himself to lend support to the project.

Securities investors, many wearing stovepipe hats of the period, jam the main hall of the Paris Bourse, or stock exchange, where they discuss the gains and losses of the daily trading activities.

During these hectic days de Lesseps rarely allowed himself to rest. His only relaxation was fencing. In the late afternoons he would return to his apartment and fence with one or another of his friends. But his work on the canal never really stopped. Business visitors would often come to see him at such times. They would knock, and the door would be flung open. And there he would be: eyes gleaming and perspiration running down his face and a sword in his hand. All in all, it was a perfect picture of de Lesseps in this time of tireless activity. He was happy and secure and playing the role he loved best, that of a man alone and defiant in the face of the world. Seeing him like this, one could not conceive of his failure.

Finally, he had made all the necessary preparations. By the beginning of November the work was done. He was ready to launch his second great attack. In England he had suffered a defeat in the diplomatic war. In France, however, he could not afford to lose the financial one.

It was de Lesseps' plan to raise the full capital for the canal by selling 400,000 shares of stock in his company. The price set for each share was five hundred francs—equivalent, at the rate of exchange of that day, to $100. To keep the ownership of the company as international as possible, he had limited the number of shares that could be sold in France to 220,000. The public subscription of stock in the canal company began on November 5, 1858, and lasted for a little more than three weeks.

As the days passed, public response was unexpected and overwhelming. The Isthmus of Suez canal had become a favorite subject and was soon on everyone's lips. In cafes, clubs, and restaurants all over France there were arguments about the wisdom of investing in the new company. Opinion was divided, and people soon took sides. Many, of course, regarded the canal as another of the great financial swindles so characteristic of the age. But others believed in de Lesseps' sincerity and were convinced that it was a good investment. True to form, those Frenchmen who favored investing in the project saw it in terms of glory for their own country, and many were motivated by strong anti-British sentiments. This was something on which de Lesseps had counted heavily. In fact, during his last conversation with Lord Palmerston in London, he had made the point very clear. "I look to your opposition," he told the Prime Minister, "as an engine for raising the capital." Nor was he wrong.

There is a story that one day, when the company stock

— Mais non! mais non! Je comprends parfaitement vo-
tre projet...
— Mais si, il faut que je vous l'explique; vous êtes l'isthme de Suez. Alors pour le percer...
— Mais non! C'est inutile, je saisis très bien!

In this contemporary cartoon, two Frenchmen argue about the canal. Although the man on the left insists he understands the project, his companion is intent on demonstrating it graphically, choosing the unlucky man's stomach to represent the isthmus and marking with a thrust of his umbrella the spot where the canal will be built.

was first put on sale, a gentleman came into the office on the Place Vendôme in a very aggressive mood. He asked to buy some shares in the new Swedish railway. His mistake was explained.

"But it is not a railway, it is a canal. It is not in Sweden, it is at Suez."

The gentleman still wanted to buy stock.

"It's all the same to me," he said. "Provided it be against the English, I subscribe."

Not everyone was so violent. But when the subscription list closed on the last day of November, almost all the shares allotted to the French market had been sold. At the final count there were more than twenty thousand Frenchmen who had seen fit to invest in a canal through the Isthmus of Suez. They had bought a total of 207,111 shares. On the whole (and this pleased de Lesseps) they were small investors who acquired an average of nine shares apiece. Less than one percent of them owned as many as 100 shares. They came from every walk of life but primarily from the middle class. Among the purchasers were lawyers

Travaux préliminaires pour le percement de l'isthme de Suez.
C'est toujours cela de commencé !

In an 1859 French cartoon, some potential investors and backers of the Suez Canal are being wined and dined. The gentlemen raise their glasses and their voices while a companion uncorks another bottle to keep their glasses filled and their spirits lifted. The caption beneath suggests that this is the way all preliminary work begins.

and engineers, doctors, teachers, and priests, bankers, merchants, and manufacturers. There were some very small investors indeed. In fact, it almost seemed that every waiter, delivery boy, and taxi driver in Paris had a share in the company. "The other day," de Lesseps said some time later, "I drove to my office in a cab, and when I had given the driver his thirty-five sous he took my hand and said, 'Monsieur de Lesseps, I am one of your shareholders.'"

English reaction to the financial launching of the company was predictably hostile. Lord Palmerston sneered that "little people have been induced to take up little shares." And the London press saw only the comic aspect of de Lesseps' success in raising a significant portion of the money. "The subscribers," one newspaper acidly noted, "are mostly waiters who have been deceived by the newspapers which they find lying around, or else they are grocers' boys . . . accustomed to read the advertisements in the old papers with which they wrap up their parcels."

But de Lesseps could afford to laugh along with these English wits. He had in his hands a little more than half the sum the engineers of the International Scientific Commission had estimated the canal would cost. From the French public alone he had received something over 100,000,000 francs ($20,000,000). And he had made provisions for raising the rest of the money in other countries. Eventually, some 10,000 additional shares were sold to a variety of foreign investors—in Spain and Holland, for example, and in Italy, Denmark, and Switzerland. Said had committed Egypt to buying a large block of almost 100,000 shares. And de Lesseps had put aside a further 85,000 shares that he planned to sell in Austria, Great Britain, Russia, and the United States. Half of the money was therefore secure, and the other half, he was confident, would soon be available. As the year 1858 came to a close, de Lesseps seemed to have every reason for optimism.

But his financial position was by no means as bright as it looked on the surface. Storm clouds were gathering. Virtually the entire block of 85,000 shares set aside by de Lesseps for sale outside of France had not been sold. The United States was not interested in a canal in the faraway Middle East. Neither, for political reasons, were Austria and Russia. And the English did not care to buy a single share. Once again, de Lesseps had made the mistake of being too optimistic; but he went ahead and incorporated the Compagnie Universelle du Canal Maritime de Suez. He announced its formation to the French Ministry of Commerce on December 26, 1858—a little over four years since Said had authorized him to form such a company.

There was an impressive sound to the company's name, but the fact remained that from a realistic point of view the stock issue was a failure. De Lesseps had raised only enough capital to get the project under way; there were few reserves for the long years of construction ahead. In fact, it turned out that the final cost of the project was more than twice the original estimate. From the moment work on the canal began, the Suez Canal Company was in financial trouble. Even though de Lesseps had raised an enormous sum of money by the end of 1858, it was not enough—and he knew it. A further source had to be found.

De Lesseps is remembered in history as a great builder. He was a great promoter as well. For, in the last analysis, the construction of the Suez Canal was not so much a feat of engineering as it was a feat of financing. The solution of the money problem was de Lesseps' finest achievement, and he accomplished it in the face of political opposition and financial apathy. Fortunately, necessity drove him from the beginning. And necessity revealed his best qualities: confidence in himself, the strength to keep going against all odds, and the ability to improvise. As the years passed and the construction costs mounted, his ability to improvise was put to the test; he passed it magnificently.

Through charm, skill, and subtle pressure he succeeded in uncovering a fantastic treasure. At the beginning it was a treasure that seemed to have no end. For nearly ten years he managed to divert a golden avalanche from the Egyptian government into the Suez Canal Company. With masterful diplomacy he persuaded not one but two rulers of Egypt to pay for the project. They were by no means easy men to deal with. Both were vain and cunning, indecisive and childish. Yet, without their lavish support, it is conceivable that the Suez Canal could be lying half-finished now, buried under the sands of the desert. It was largely owing to de Lesseps' manipulations that two Egyptian viceroys

The 500-franc share issued by the Suez Canal Company has a special Egyptian flavor. The certificate is written both in Arabic and in French, and its margins contain highly romantic scenes of Egypt.

محمد سعيد پاشا پاشة مصر
توفي في اسكندريه في ١٧ يناير
سنه ١٨٦٢ ميلاديه
مطابقة هجريه

became the guardian angels of the canal. Said and his successor, his nephew Ismail Pasha, supplied all the money he needed—sometimes willingly and sometimes not.

Between them they had the dubious distinction of saving the canal and destroying their own country in the process. For the creation of the Suez Canal and the financial disintegration of Egypt began at almost the same moment. In 1854, when de Lesseps first visited Said, the country was enjoying the stable government passed on by Mohammed Ali. It was prosperous and without debt. But by the time the canal was completed in 1869, the Egyptian government owed money to every banker in Europe and was on the edge of financial ruin. It is true that not all of the money had been spent on the Suez Canal. Yet there is no doubt that it was largely responsible for the country's bankruptcy. Although there was perhaps no other way to build the canal, given the nature of the project and the nature of the personalities involved, the financial plight of Egypt was a melancholy black mark against de Lesseps and his company.

De Lesseps' old friend and patron Said was the first to start down the reckless road that led to Egypt's ruin, and de Lesseps was there to help him along the way. At the beginning, Said's commitment to the canal was a small one. He had paid the expenses of the International Scientific Commission, which made the preliminary survey of the isthmus in 1855. Since that time he had given de Lesseps 500,000 francs ($100,000) a year to pay for public relations. In addition, he was underwriting a monthly journal, *L'Isthme de Suez*, which de Lesseps published for propaganda purposes. These minor expenses seemed justified since the Egyptian government stood to gain 15 per cent of the company's future profits from toll charges. And an enormous amount of shipping was expected to pass through the canal. Actually, Said had committed his government to no more than providing the necessary land on the isthmus and supplying workmen, who were to be paid by the company.

This happy state of affairs did not last for very long. As the years passed, de Lesseps managed to involve Said more and more in the financial problems of the company. When the stock issue was floated in 1858, Said grandly promised

Surrounded by symbols of ancient and modern Egypt, Said, in a portrait made a year before he died, reveals a drooping right eyelid and a tired face.

to buy almost 100,000 shares. And, eventually, de Lesseps persuaded him to guarantee in addition the shares that had been reserved for the United States, Austria, Russia, and Great Britain. So it turned out, in spite of de Lesseps' insistence on the international character of the project, that the French public paid for half the shares, and Egypt— through Said—promised to pay for the other half. Only about 10,000 shares were in the hands of other investors. The Viceroy's ego was largely responsible for his grandiose commitment to the canal. Less than a month after the first shares had been put on the market, he explained his position to the British consul at Cairo, who was trying to persuade him to turn against de Lesseps.

"People are mistaken in Europe," announced Said, "if they attribute the piercing of the isthmus to Monsieur de Lesseps alone, for I am the promoter of it. Monsieur de Lesseps has merely carried out my instructions."

De Lesseps was more than careful not to disillusion him on this point. To find the money for his unthinking commitments, Said began to borrow from European bankers. In a short time these pledges, added to his extravagance and the high interest rate of the loans, had created a national debt of around 400,000,000 francs ($80,000,000).

During the critical money-raising period after 1856, de Lesseps' monthly journal (opposite) kept the project in the public eye. A profile of the southern half of the Isthmus of Suez (below) includes two areas of rocky terrain through which the canal would pass north of Mer Rouge (Red Sea)—Shallufa Ridge (left) and Serapeum Ridge (far right). The large depression is the area of the Bitter Lakes.
(continued on page 98)

F. DE LESSEPS, *Percement de l'Isthme de Suez*

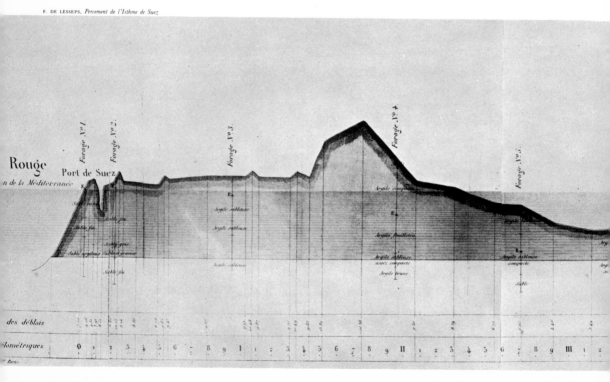

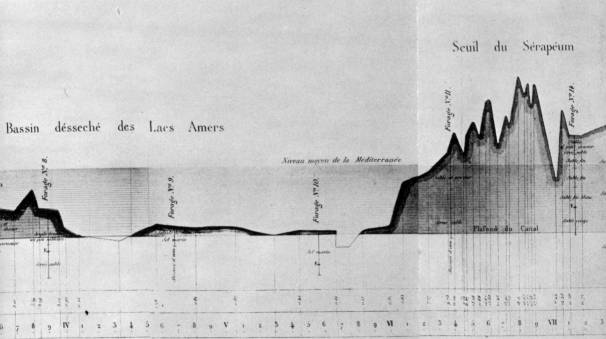

It was Egypt's first such debt. When Said died in 1863, the financial burden was passed on to his successor.

Yet the burden did not seem to bother Ismail Pasha in the least. He was, in every way, more extreme than his uncle Said. He was also impulsive and fond of luxury. His delusions of grandeur were extensive, and he managed to persuade the sultan of Turkey to give him a more impressive title than Viceroy—in 1867 he became Khedive of Egypt. Of greater interest to de Lesseps, Ismail was as involved in the building of the Suez Canal as Said, and he was even more extravagant than his uncle. Ismail developed more projects to increase his prestige than simply the canal. It was his ambition to turn his capital city of Cairo into the Paris of the Middle East. To this end he started a program of modernization. He built wide boulevards and parks, a magnificent new opera house, and one luxurious palace after another. The transformation of Cairo—not to mention the construction of the Suez Canal—required spectacular sums of money. Casually, and with no thought for the future, Ismail borrowed from the European bankers at increasingly higher rates of interest.

For all his extravagance and despotic nature, Ismail Pasha was a charming man, though his attractive person-

The conspicuously flat northern profile of the isthmus from Lake Timsah to the Mediterranean (far right) is broken only by the rocky peaks of El Jisr, to the left of Lake Ballah. The shallow waters of Lake Manzala make up almost one quarter of the isthmus' length.

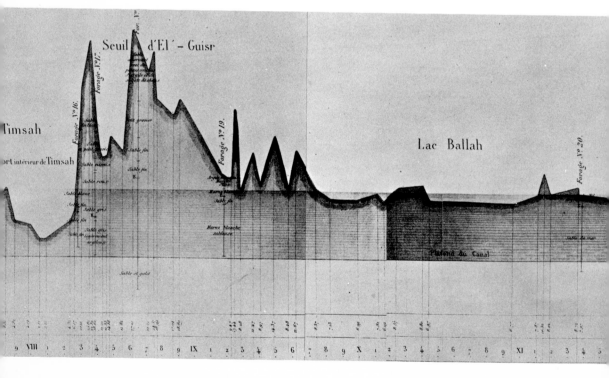

ality was somewhat obscured by an unkempt appearance that was far from regal. His beard was red and uncombed, and one eyelid drooped in a distracting fashion. Short and plump, he shuffled through his various palaces like a trained bear. He habitually wore a crimson fez that appeared several sizes too large for him, and he was in the habit of receiving his visitors while sitting cross-legged on a divan, Turkish fashion. At such times Ismail was given to playing with his toes in an absorbed manner and rolling his eyes in opposite directions. It was all most disconcerting. But, no doubt, he was lost in a world of his own, meditating on further ways to spend money. His extravagances were unlimited, and eventually they led to his banishment by the sultan of Turkey.

This move, however, came too late, for Ismail had managed to plunge his country into debt at the staggering rate of 200,000,000 francs ($40,000,000) a year. Roughly 20 per cent of this money was spent on the construction of the Suez Canal and included all the lavish expenses of its opening celebrations. Despite this ultimate ruin to himself and to his country, there is no doubt that Ismail, guided by the clever hand of de Lesseps, was the single most important contributor to the financing of the Suez Canal.

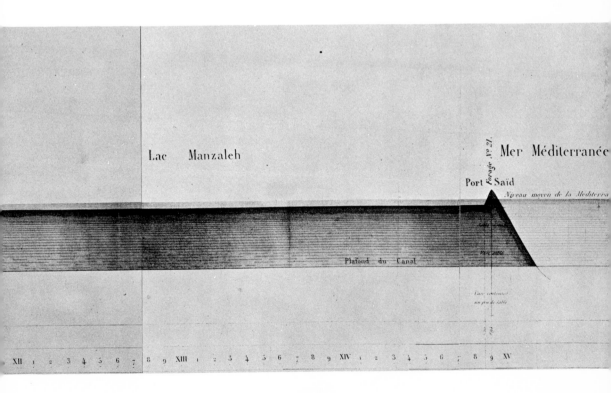

An enthusiastic crowd, including a deputation from Said (far right), greets de Lesseps (right of center, underneath the small flag) upon his arrival in Alexandria after a promotional tour around Europe. The words on the banner describe the sentiments of the delegation.

At the beginning of 1859—just after the close of the public subscription in France—de Lesseps returned to Egypt. The Egyptian treasury had not yet been opened to him, and the golden stream that would eventually flow from Said and Ismail was hidden in the future. Looking at the cold figures, de Lesseps saw that he had raised only half of the necessary amount. The remainder lay in the vague promises of Said. But he faced the problem with characteristic impulsiveness. He made up his

mind to go ahead and begin the construction of the canal.

So the last act had begun. He was ready to start work on the canal that had been his dream for twenty-five years. With the chief engineers, Linant Bey and Mougel Bey, he led a handful of workmen to the shores of Lake Manzala at the Mediterranean end of the Isthmus of Suez.

On a narrow strip of land separating the lake from the Bay of Pelusium, the new canal was started. Here the engineers planned to build an artificial harbor and with it a

101

An informal ceremony at Port Said (opposite) officially begins canal construction. Ferdinand de Lesseps (fourth from left, with pick in hand) is
ignored by laborers already at work as he prepares to break the symbolic
first dirt. Above, railroad tracks lead to an equipment dump at Port Said;
beyond, work progresses on the construction of a temporary wooden jetty.

town for warehouses, living quarters, and company offices. The harbor was of the greatest importance, for it marked the northern end of the canal and its point of entry into the Mediterranean. De Lesseps called it Port Said; it seemed the least he could do for the Viceroy.

On the morning of April 25, 1859, four merchant ships anchored in the Bay of Pelusium and started unloading supplies for the first phases of construction. There was timber for a temporary jetty, along with engineering equipment and material for building a lighthouse. Not far away, on the shores of Lake Manzala, a small group was gathered around two wooden stakes that had been driven into the desert. A string between them marked the exact spot where the canal was to begin. Bending over, de Lesseps picked up a shovel and dug into the sand. Then he passed the shovel on to his engineering staff and to each of the hundred workmen standing by. One by one they turned over a shovelful of sand. In such a way, quietly and without drama, the Suez Canal was begun.

The sun burned in the sky. De Lesseps shaded his eyes and looked across the lake, toward the south, toward Suez. He could see the last hundred miles of his long journey. There seemed to be only one enemy now—the hostile desert, waiting in silence beyond the lake.

VI THE SAND GIANT

There is a story told that soon after the first digging at Port Said, de Lesseps came upon a solitary Egyptian workman far out in the marshes of Lake Manzala.

"Good morning, my friend," said de Lesseps. "What are you doing here?"

"Can't you see I'm building the Suez Canal?" said the worker with some irritation, pointing to the shovel in his hand.

This solitary workman, equipped with no more than a shovel and a palm-leaf basket, defines the extent of de Lesseps' optimism in 1859. Surely it required a kind of insane courage for him to begin the project at all. True, a few cubic feet of sand had been turned over, but there were

Mechanical dredgers floating on rafts widen and deepen the channel as laborers with wheelbarrows haul soil to build up the canal banks.

a hundred million more to dig before the canal reached Suez and the Red Sea. There was not enough money to finish the job, and little heavy equipment was available. De Lesseps was beginning the battle against the desert with no more than the bare hands of his workmen. His salvation lay in an unshakable belief that the future would take care of itself. That it actually did was the result of a great deal of luck and of an engineering plan notable for its simplicity.

The method of attack proposed by de Lesseps and his engineers was basically, and deceptively, simple. It was fortunate that less than half of the canal's one hundred miles had to be carved out of the sand. In plotting its

The first part of the fresh-water canal (gray line) from Zagazig, on a Nile tributary, to Lake Timsah was finished in February, 1862. The southern branch to Suez paralleled the Maritime Canal (white line); it was completed in the same year. An extension to Cairo, providing a more abundant supply of Nile water, and a pipeline branch to Port Said (broken line) were completed in time for the 1869 opening.

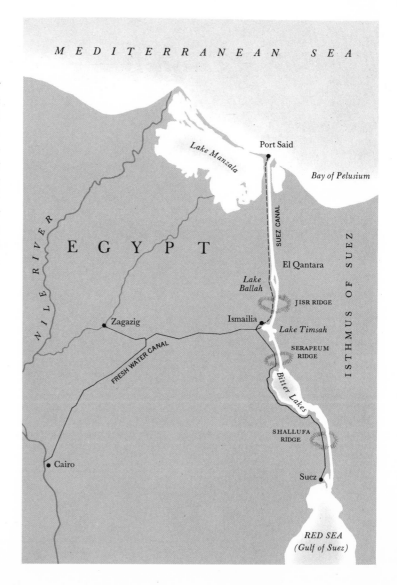

Illustrated London News

Soil to be carried from the excavation is shoveled by native Egyptian workmen, the fellahin, *into baskets slung over the backs of camels.*

course, de Lesseps' engineers had taken every advantage of the five desert lakes that lay on the isthmus between Port Said and Suez. With the exception of Lake Manzala, which was marshy and filled with water, these lakes were dry. Lake Timsah, Lake Ballah, and the Great Bitter and Little Bitter lakes were arid, salt-encrusted depressions in the sand. De Lesseps' design was simple: to link this chain of lakes by stretches of canal and fill them with sea water. The connected links were to be the Suez Canal.

The success of this plan required that one team of workmen push the canal south from Port Said to the dry basin of Lake Timsah and bring water from the Mediterranean into it. Another team had to cut north from Suez and fill the Bitter Lakes with water from the Red Sea. The difficult passage through Lake Manzala aside, there was less than forty miles of sand through which the completed canal

Huge stone blocks form a break-water (below) to protect the canal entrance at Port Said from violent sea currents. By contrast, the placid fresh-water canal (right) flows past foliage-covered banks.

must pass. The task, however, was by no means as easy as it appeared on the blueprints.

Along the route stood three spectacular ridges of rock and sand. The first was the Jisr Ridge, a formidable plateau some ten miles long and thirty feet above sea level. It blocked the way into Lake Timsah. Between Timsah and the Bitter Lakes was the Serapeum Ridge, a similar barrier of rock and sand. Thirteen miles north of Suez, standing at the southern approach to the Bitter Lakes, was the natural wall at Shallufa—the greatest obstacle of them all. The problems of digging through these ridges without the proper machinery were enormous. Shallufa, for example, remained a problem until the very day the canal opened.

BOTH: *Illustrated London News*

Before the actual digging of the canal itself could be started, there were two immediate problems facing de Lesseps and his engineers. First, an unlimited supply of fresh water had to be made available. Second, an artificial harbor had to be built at Port Said.

Fresh water was essential in any attack on the desert. Without it there could be no towns and harbors at Port Said, Lake Timsah, or Suez. Natural wells were almost nonexistent on the isthmus, and the amount of rain water that could be collected was not sufficient for a work force that soon numbered in the thousands. Even though the canal itself was to reach below the water line in many places, such a source would contain brackish water and would by no means be dependable.

So a canal to carry fresh water to the isthmus was begun at Zagazig, in the Nile Valley north of Cairo. From there it was to cut across the desert and run parallel to the Suez Canal from Port Said to Suez. Said, honoring the terms of the Second Concession, provided Egyptian laborers for the task. With shovels, baskets, and bare hands they dug across the Wadi Tumilat, following the route of the canal of the pharaohs. It was slow work, and not until early 1862 did they reach Timsah and begin turning the stream of fresh water north to Port Said and south to Suez. Meanwhile, water came by ship to the area of Port Said and by camel back to the other stations along the way. At every work site it was put into casks and closely watched over by Egyptian soldiers.

As the fresh-water canal inched toward the Isthmus of Suez, a great new harbor was growing at Port Said. It was essential to have adequate facilities for unloading construction equipment, food, medicine, and other supplies. Before long the temporary jetty had been replaced by two stone breakwaters that reached out into the Mediterranean, creating an anchorage for the large ships that would eventually pass through the completed Suez Canal. A safe anchorage was most important since this part of the Egyptian coast, open to a prevailing northwest wind, was treacherous and ran with strong currents. The breakwaters—one, two thousand yards long, and the other, three thousand—were formed by lowering huge blocks of stone into the sea. In the end there were thirty thousand of them, each weighing more than twenty tons. Some of the blocks came by ship from quarries west of Alexandria, and others were made on the spot by mixing lime with sea water and sand. In addition to the construction of these breakwaters, the harbor itself had to be dredged to a greater depth. Between 1859 and 1862 other work was in various stages of progress. The lighthouse was rising brick by brick, and the town of Port Said was taking shape on a tongue of land (almost, in fact, an island) that separated Lake Manzala from the Mediterranean.

Once these harbor works were under way and the freshwater canal from Cairo started, de Lesseps was free to concentrate on his major problem—cutting a channel through the isthmus and joining the Mediterranean to the Red Sea. As a basis for the future Suez Canal a preliminary ditch had to be dug from Port Said to Suez. Called the service canal, it had two functions: to provide a way of floating machinery and supplies down to Suez and to sketch out the course of the completed waterway. Though the service canal was never more than twenty feet wide and six feet deep, it was the embryo of the Suez Canal.

The first obstacle through which the service canal had to pass was Lake Manzala, a shallow lake that covered the thirty miles between Port Said and the beginning of the desert at El Qantara. It was not really a lake at all, but an extended lagoon, varying in depth from three to four feet. Digging through this uncertain swamp a channel that could hold water presented many difficulties. All initial excavations were done by hand, and the work was frustrating. At the beginning the mud and slime seemed insurmountable obstacles.

The Egyptian workmen, however, were used to the isthmus and dealt with this barrier in a primitive but effective way. They scooped armfuls of dripping mud from the lake bottom and squeezed them to their chests. Then they put the mud out to dry in the sun on both sides of the small ditch they had managed to form. It

L'Illustration

Scaffolding surrounds the towering fifty-foot-high lighthouse under construction at Port Said harbor.

COMPAGNIE FINANCIERE DE SUEZ, PARIS

Men aided by a camel pull supply boats along the first narrow traces of the canal in Lake Manzala.

was a slow method: only when one layer of mud was dry could they put another on top of it. In this way, earthen banks held back the swamp on either side of a shallow new waterway. As the Egyptians labored through the morass, mechanical dredgers followed in their wake. These machines (at the time there were only four of them in Port Said) widened the channel and deepened it until they reached the hard clay under the mud. Then they poured this clay on top of the banks that had been started by the laborers. Layer by layer the banks rose, and the sun baked them into a rocklike hardness. Soon they were six feet high and solid enough to provide roads over which supplies could be moved. Heavier equipment could be floated in the service canal itself, into which Mediterranean water now flowed.

With no more than hand labor and a few machines, de Lesseps had started his great waterway. In the face of many difficulties he had built a firm and dry service canal through the marshy bottom of Lake Manzala. This narrow channel marked out the first thirty miles of the canal, but

111

Et. CARJ

seventy more miles lay ahead—through the desert, the dry lakes, and the ridges of sand and rock at Jisr, Serapeum, and Shallufa. In conquering Lake Manzala, de Lesseps had overcome only one of the great natural barriers that blocked the path of his canal.

The work was endlessly slow. There were daily failures and frustrations. The engineering problem by itself was discouraging enough. In addition, de Lesseps was having serious difficulties with the Viceroy. Now that actual construction had started, Said was far from happy. For the first time he was beginning to worry about the opposition of the sultan of Turkey, who still had not given approval to the project. Uncertainty led the Viceroy to grow cool toward de Lesseps. He created unnecessary red tape and sent various officials to the area of Lake Manzala in order to obstruct the works. At one point he ordered all construction to stop. Then he reversed the decision. De Lesseps saw that something had to be done to calm the nervous monarch. So he played his last strong card. And he won.

For nearly five years he had been trying to persuade Napoleon III to give official French support to the canal.

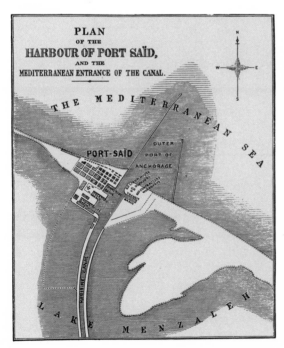
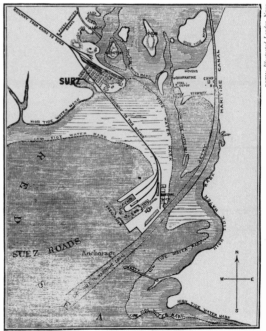

A French cartoonist makes de Lesseps into a gigantic Samson whose strength has pushed apart the earth and opened a canal (opposite). Above, plans of Port Said (left) and Suez (right) show the two entry points into the canal.

De Lesseps (fourth from left) and three colleagues casually lounge in flowing Arab robes. Posing in a more sedate manner is M. Borel, one of the canal's chief engineers.

He had relied heavily on Eugénie to bring this about. But Napoleon III wanted no trouble with England, and despite his wife's intercessions on behalf of de Lesseps, had delayed coming to any decision. By the end of 1859, however, the Emperor was feeling more arrogant and less in awe of the British Empire. He had just emerged victoriously from the Crimean War and was casting about for other ways to increase the glory of France. And here was the Suez Canal actually under construction, a new path to the Orient and a possible source of French prestige in the Middle East. On October 23, 1859 (after much prodding by Eugénie), the Emperor summoned de Lesseps to St. Cloud, the royal residence near Paris. There was an important question on Napoleon's mind.

"How is it, Monsieur de Lesseps," he asked, "that so many people are against your enterprise?"

De Lesseps did not hesitate to tell the truth. "Your Majesty, it is because they think you will not stand by me."

The Emperor twisted the tips of his mustache and

The Grand Hotel d'Orient, de Lesseps' home in Cairo during much of the construction period, overlooks the lively Place Esbekyeh.

smiled. "Well, do not be uneasy," he said at last. "You may count on my assistance and protection."

De Lesseps was overjoyed. At last he had the strong political ally his project needed. The news of Napoleon's decision calmed the vacillating Said, and he did not, for the moment, put further obstacles in de Lesseps' way.

Hurrying back to Port Said, de Lesseps threw himself into the work with greater energy than before. Against the stark background of the isthmus all the complexities and sophistications of Europe vanished. They were no more substantial than desert mirages.

For de Lesseps the physical work of the canal became the only reality. In the desert he acted out the greatest role of his life, taking his place as field commander of a fantastic enterprise. During the course of construction there were times when he was responsible for as many as fifty thousand people and millions of francs' worth of equipment. The days and the months passed, and he ranged back and forth along the length of the isthmus—pushing, encouraging, and praising his engineering staff and workers. He was well into his fifties, but he managed to summon up the energy and the vitality of a man half his age. Mounted on a fast pony, he seemed to be everywhere at once. With his sleeves turned up and a sun helmet on his head or dressed in a billowing Arab burnoose, he sweated and worked each day along with his men.

By 1862 he had pushed the service canal through Lake Manzala and into the desert past El Qantara. Persistence

and the labor of thousands of Egyptians had carved a passable channel through the great Jisr Ridge. On November 18, 1862, water from the Mediterranean flowed into the dry basin of Lake Timsah. The narrow ribbon of the service canal had been brought almost half way down to Suez.

At this stage there were many reasons for de Lesseps to be optimistic. A clear stencil of the Suez Canal had been cut from Port Said to Lake Timsah, and the fresh-water canal had reached the area as well. Construction had been under way for only three years, and these were impressive accomplishments. Very real progress had been made in the face of brutal difficulties of climate and terrain.

One did not have to be an engineer to see that the canal would be finished after all. Even a diplomat could see it. Sir Henry Bulwer, the British ambassador to Constantinople, came to the isthmus at the end of 1862, gathering facts for the Foreign Office. The British government still counted on de Lesseps' failure and the collapse of the entire scheme. But Sir Henry was obliged to report that it would be entirely wrong to "underrate what has been done and overrate the remaining difficulties." Here was a grudging admission that the Suez Canal was, finally and securely, in the realm of fact. It was no longer an eccentric dream or a remote possibility. On a day in the future, water would flow through it, and ships laden with cargo would pass between its banks.

Yet progress on the great canal was not quite as impressive as it seemed at first glance. By 1862 little beyond preliminary harbor works at Suez had been done in the south. The stubborn ridge at Shallufa continued to resist every assault upon it. True, the service canal had reached Lake Timsah, but the work already had cost 50,000,000 francs ($10,000,000), a quarter of the actual cash in hand. And less than 10 per cent of the sand that blocked the canal's path had been removed. At this rate of digging it would take from fifteen to twenty years to complete the full hundred miles of the job.

More important, a point had been reached in the excavations where the service canal had to be widened and deepened extensively. A narrow ditch, twenty feet wide and six feet deep, had to be turned into a waterway capable of carrying ocean-going vessels. Picks and shovels and bare hands were no longer enough, nor was de Lesseps' blind faith in the future.

The work, in order to be finished in any reasonable time, demanded heavy machinery. As usual, there was not

The dazzling array of medals worn by Ismail Pasha in the portrait at left attests to his affection for ostentatious display. Ismail, like his predecessor, Mohammed Said, did little to alleviate the distressing conditions and the injustices suffered by the impoverished of his realm, for his mind and his money centered on self-indulgent whims. Opposite, poor vendors huddle together in a Cairo bazaar not far from the ruler's splendid palace.

enough money to buy it, and another entry was added to de Lesseps' long catalogue of financial woes. Luck, however, was still on his side. From a surprising corner there came a miraculous solution. Ironically, the moral indignation of England was to be his salvation.

It was an unpleasant fact that the workmen supplied by Said were, in all but name, slaves. For two years he had been maintaining a force of twenty thousand Egyptian laborers on the isthmus. Forced labor was nothing new in Egypt. From the time of the pharaohs Egyptian peasants had been called from their villages to construct public works; they had no choice in the matter. Said's huge labor force was convenient and cheap. Wages were small, food was poor, and the incentive to work was always the lash. Such forced labor had built the new harbor at Alexandria and had worked on the Cairo-to-Suez railroad. In the past

Illustrated London News

The quiet desert bustled with activity during canal construction. Above, camels and their drivers, carrying a cargo of boilers across the isthmus, rest at an oasis. Below, a dismantled dredge is lugged across the desert to the canal site.

no one in the rest of the world had given much thought to what Egyptians did to other Egyptians. But the Suez Canal was a European enterprise and almost exclusively a French one at that. A political storm developed around the fact that the canal was being built by conscript labor. The world was shocked that Egyptians were dying in the desert from heat, overwork, and cholera.

It was, on the surface, an ugly picture. Politicians in England, spurred on by various societies for the abolition of slavery, made the most of it. They condemned de Lesseps and his company, and the temper of the times was in their favor. Freedom was very much in the air. On the other side of the world the United States was engaged in a civil war over slavery, and President Abraham Lincoln had delivered his Emancipation Proclamation in January, 1863. Yet the outcry against de Lesseps had been raised in England as much from a desire to stop work on the canal as from humanitarian motives. Diplomatic pressure was brought to bear on Constantinople, and the sultan of Turkey ordered Ismail Pasha, the new ruler of Egypt (Said had died in the first month of 1863), to withdraw all laborers from the isthmus. In the spring of 1864, work in the desert came to a halt, and the construction sites along the canal were strangely silent.

Without Egyptian laborers de Lesseps could do nothing. He had no money to hire others, let alone buy the heavy machinery required to complete the canal. Moreover, Ismail, the sultan, and others were now attempting to wrest control of the canal from him. Hoping to enlist

L'Illustration

Napoleon III on their side, they asked the Emperor for an impartial ruling on the labor problem.

Napoleon, however, decided that Ismail owed the company money as compensation for the loss of its labor force. He felt that under the terms of the two acts of concession the Egyptian government had guaranteed to supply workers for the canal. The final figure, awarded to the company in August, 1864, was 84,000,000 francs ($16,800,000).

So de Lesseps emerged as the winner, and Ismail, in a financial sense, was the loser. He was now well launched on his extravagant course of paying for the Suez Canal. He paid now, and he would continue to pay in the future. Out of near disaster, de Lesseps had managed to pluck an enormous sum of money, and at the precise moment when he needed it to buy machinery.

The way was now clear to Suez. In the summer of 1864, work on the canal began again, and de Lesseps was free to continue his journey in the clean, dry air of the desert. Construction moved ahead at an astonishing pace. And it did not slow down until the morning—five years later—when Eugénie's yacht steamed through the canal.

By 1865 construction was entering an entirely new phase. The amateur days of pick and shovel were over. During the next four years, professionals moved in to complete the job. With the money extracted from Ismail as a result of Napoleon III's decision, de Lesseps could well

A cartoonist lampoons the halting of work in 1864—the Egyptian Viceroy stalks off with the tools.

OVERLEAF: *The release of Mediterranean water into Timsah is accompanied by ceremonial fanfare.*

Dredgers afloat in canal waters
were functional if rather bizarre-
looking machines. The photograph
and diagram opposite show the profile of a typical dredger—buckets
attached to a conveyer system scoop
up mud from the canal bed. At left,
the elevateur deposits buckets of
dredged-up mud on the banks.
Above, visitors inspect a dredger.

afford to pay them. Perhaps Ismail derived some comfort from the fact that the halfway station at Lake Timsah was to be named Ismailia in his honor.

At this stage of construction the principal contracting work was being done by the French firm of Borel and Lavalley. In consultation with de Lesseps and the director of engineering, Voisin Bey, the contractors designed and built an enormous fleet of mechanical dredgers and steam excavators. At the peak of their operations these machines generated some ten thousand horsepower and were capable of digging out the canal at the rate of six million cubic feet a month. With these powerful machines at work it was hard to remember the Egyptian workmen and their palm-leaf baskets and their naked struggle against the desert.

With impressive speed the dredgers began to widen and deepen the service canal that stretched from Port Said to Lake Timsah and beyond. The machines came in many different sizes, and most of them were invented specifically for the Suez Canal project. No precedent for the dredgers existed, since the world had never seen an engineering problem of this type and magnitude. Run by steam engines, the machines were set up on barges in the canal. From wooden towers an endless chain of buckets scooped mud from the canal bottom. Long chutes deposited the mud on the banks of the canal or onto other barges that carried it out to sea—whether at Port Said or at Suez. By 1869 these giant machines had succeeded in enlarging the service canal to the point where it could accommodate ocean-going vessels. On opening day the Suez Canal was

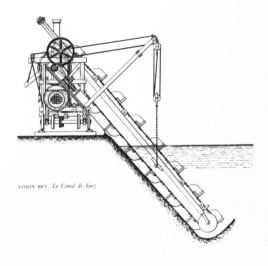

VOISIN BEY, *Le Canal de Suez*

26 feet deep, with a minimum bottom width of 72 feet and a surface width of some 175 feet.

The last year of work on the isthmus was one of unending activity. While the dredgers plied the canal, harbors and new towns were being completed at Port Said, Ismailia, and Suez. The fresh-water canal was being extended all along the line. Even at night the work went on, lighted by resinous wood burning in overhead grills.

No one worked as hard as de Lesseps himself during these last frantic months of construction. He moved con-

stantly back and forth along the whole hundred miles of the
canal from Port Said to Suez. There was no work site he did
not inspect and no problem of rock or sand he did not face
himself. Often he was called to Cairo to help Ismail with
plans for the opening celebrations. Lights burned into the
night in de Lesseps' personal villa at Ismailia, where he
pored over daily engineering reports. He was a man past
sixty, but he never slowed his pace.

Happily, his problems were vanishing. Money was
available to him in a way that it had never been before,

A symbolic last pickaxe is flourished (center) in the presence of Ali Pasha, Turkey's grand vizier, and other distinguished guests who have come to witness the opening of the dike that held back the Red Sea waters from the Bitter Lakes.

and all his machines were working at a fever pace. Even the great danger of sand filling the canal and making the work impossible had never materialized. The sand, mixed with sea water, had turned into a firm and cohesive paste. And at the bottom of the channel the dredgers had come up against material almost the consistency of sandstone. The canal was firm, and it would hold. De Lesseps had won the battle against the sand giant.

And he had won his battle against England too. Death had removed his great enemy Lord Palmerston in 1865. Less than a year later came the long-awaited permission from Constantinople. On March 19, 1866, the sultan of Turkey gave his belated blessings to the Suez Canal.

Still there were heartbreaking barriers. There was, for example, the stubborn ledge of rock at Shallufa, which had been a problem from the very beginning. It held the Red Sea back from the Bitter Lakes, which had been filled with Mediterranean water since 1868. Desperately, with picks, shovels, and machines, de Lesseps and his workmen attacked the rock formation at Shallufa. It was the summer of 1869, and invitations for the opening ceremonies on November 17 had already been sent out.

Finally it was conquered. On August 15, 1869, the Red Sea flowed along the channel from Suez and poured into the Bitter Lakes, blending with water from the Mediterranean. The two seas had been joined, and East and West were one. In October a French steamer made the first complete transit of the canal by an ocean-going vessel. Within a month the Suez Canal would be open to the world.

Yet the last month was one of near disaster for de Lesseps. On November 2 another ledge of rock was discovered in the channel that went through the murderous Shallufa Ridge. The ships that were even now beginning to fill the harbor at Port Said for the opening celebrations would never be able to sail past it.

"Go and get powder at Cairo," ordered de Lesseps. "Masses of powder. And, then, if we cannot blow up the rock, we will blow ourselves up!"

Dynamite cleared the channel, and the crisis passed. But on November 15 a great fire broke out at Port Said in a lumber yard where fireworks had been stored. It took two thousand Egyptian soldiers to save the docks and warehouses from destruction. Still the ordeal was not over. On November 16—the day before the opening—an Egyptian corvette, scouting the way for the great procession, ran aground in the channel near El Qantara. All Khedive

At Port Said's canal entrance, a banner-waving crowd watches the arrival of ships participating in the opening-day festivities.

Ismail's magnificent plans for the opening celebrations hung in the balance. Ismail himself rushed to the scene and directed the refloating of the stricken ship.

Finally, on the morning of November 17, 1869, all machinery ground to a stop, and the workmen put down their tools. One man's magnificent dream had become a reality at last. The cannon sounded and the bands played and the Empress of the French led a line of ships past the entrance to the Suez Canal. The incredible journey had begun.

De Lesseps was with the Empress on the bridge of her yacht, *l'Aigle*. It was the moment he had dreamed of for nearly forty years. But once the procession had started through Lake Manzala, he went below to his cabin. There is a report that he slept all the way to Ismailia.

OVERLEAF: *An artist's panoramic view of the isthmus after the completion of the Suez Canal shows a crowded waterway reaching from the Suez roadstead (foreground) north to the Mediterranean horizon. To the west, the Nile River's tributaries and branches meander through the fertile delta to the sea.*

BIBLIOTECA DEL CIVICO MUSEO DI BELLE ARTI, TRIESTE

VII

WHERE TWO WORLDS MEET

As the year 1870 began, the warehouses at Port Said were filling with exotic merchandise from all the bazaars of the Far East. In the busy streets of the new town on the Mediterranean one could smell the unfamiliar odors of distant cities—the spices of Canton and the curries of Delhi and Benares. A heavy scent of jasmine and sandalwood hung in the air. Once again, after eleven centuries, goods were being carried by water from West to East and from East to West over the Isthmus of Suez. De Lesseps' magnificent new highway to the Orient was in full operation. Two seas had been joined and with them two worlds, and a desert wilderness had become a green and pleasant land.

Fresh water played in the fountains of the Place de Lesseps at Port Said, and little towns had grown up all along the route of the canal. At Ismailia there were brightly painted villas and lovely gardens. Flowers bloomed along the great Shallufa barrier. The fresh-water canal, cutting across the sand from Cairo, was filled with steam launches and gay pleasure boats. Acacias, orange trees, and green grass grew in places where only a few years before there had been nothing but the endless desert. The canal itself teemed with fish. Curiously, they stayed in their own familiar waters. Those from the Mediterranean swam in Lake Timsah and in the channel leading north to Port Said. Fish from the Red Sea stayed in the Bitter Lakes and in the canal down to Suez.

The extravagant opening celebrations were over, and the kings and emperors had departed. An English traveler,

The spreading branches of a tree frame a freighter and a small tug passing each other in Suez Canal waters near Ismailia. This peaceful contemporary scene is in sharp contrast to much of the canal's stormy history.

133

going through the canal at the beginning of the first year, reported that "all was quiet, sleepy, dull." It was hard to remember de Lesseps' brutal and violent struggle against the desert. But there was an enormous amount of work still to be done. The canal was by no means finished. Dredgers worked constantly to widen and deepen the canal, work that is going on even today. There were, in addition, many finishing touches to be made. The side slopes of the canal had to be paved against the danger of the banks sliding into the water, and wooden barriers had to be erected to keep sand from drifting into the channel. Naturally, these improvements added to the final cost of the canal, which was approaching 500,000,000 francs ($100,000,000).

Yet de Lesseps felt that the cost of the canal and all the difficulties endured in the building of it were in the end more than justified. He was not alone in this opinion. Even in England the Suez Canal came to be regarded as one of the wonders of the nineteenth century. De Lesseps himself became a hero, and his canal was given full coverage in the newspapers of the world. To readers in London, Paris, and New York, his exploit was no less daring that a present-

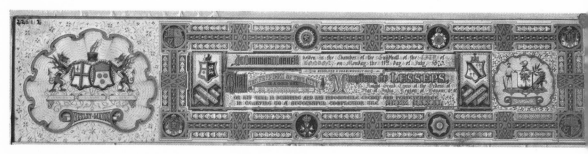

BOTH: MUSEE DE CHATEAUROUX

In July, 1870, de Lesseps was honored by the city of London with a certificate (above) granting him the freedom of the city; the elegant gold casket at left held the award. His later years were further cheered by his marriage in 1869 to his second wife, Hélène de Bragard. Opposite, she and de Lesseps pose with nine of their eleven children. But his attempts to build a canal in Panama, begun in 1879, when he was seventy-four years old, ended in defeat.

day orbit of the globe. For his too had been a voyage into space. He had reduced the distance between Europe and the Far East by over five thousand miles and had reopened a forgotten avenue of trade. De Lesseps became the best-known Frenchman of his day, and his praises were heard in every language. Perhaps the peak of his triumph was reached on July 3, 1871, when the queen of England presented him with the Order of the Star of India. The symbolic nature of this honor was lost on no one. For the moment, France, England, and the East were joined in harmonious friendship.

The canal was far-reaching in its significance. Not only did it re-establish an ancient pattern of trade but it was destined to affect the history of commerce for a hundred years to come. In ever increasing quantities raw materials from the Orient were carried to the industrial centers of Europe. Finished products were returned in the other direction. No merchant ship had to face the long and difficult voyage around the Cape of Good Hope. The new route was shorter, safer, and far cheaper. With each year that passed, the tempo of trade flowing through the Suez Canal in-

Conférence de Constantinople

creased. In 1870 under five thousand ships used it. In modern times, as many as twenty thousand vessels have passed through the waterway in a single year. In the century since the canal opened there has been an almost constant movement of ships between Port Said and Suez.

In war, as in peace, all nations have been free to use the canal and pay its toll charges. The Convention of Constantinople, signed by nine nations in 1888, was a guarantee that the Suez Canal would be open to "every vessel of commerce or of war, without distinction of flag." And so it has been, with rare exceptions, to the present day. In 1905

136

Constantinople was the setting for an 1885 conference of European and Turkish diplomats, one of several at which the affairs of Egypt were discussed. The bushy-haired secretary (extreme right at the smaller table) drew this caricature of the meeting.

Russia sent her fleet through the canal to the disastrous war with Japan. In 1935 the Italian government paid for the passage of troops to East Africa in order to mount the invasion of Ethiopia. But, if the canal has been used for war, it has been used more often for peaceful commerce.

During—and long after—the canal's opening, there were many toasts drunk in champagne and much talk of it bringing international harmony and lasting peace to the world. Certainly this was the aspect of the Suez Canal that most appealed to de Lesseps. The commercial and financial aspects meant little to him. Beyond a reasonable salary he took as president of the company, he made little from the whole project. In an age of materialism he was an idealist; he was fond of explaining his concept of the Suez Canal with a favorite Latin phrase: *Aperire terram gentibus*, "To open the world to all people." For him these words justified the forty years of his life spent in dreaming of the canal and working toward its completion.

Certainly the nature of the canal's location made it a unique instrument for bringing about peace and understanding. It stood at the crossroad of two worlds and had an infinite capacity to foster friendship between nations. Unfortunately, it had an infinite capacity to alienate them as well. And this depressing paradox has marked the whole course of the canal's history. Commercially, it has been a magnificent success. Politically, it has been a disaster for much of its history. Of the three countries most involved—England, France, and Egypt—Egypt may be said to have received the most benefit from it. If this is so, it is one of the nicer ironies of history.

For at the beginning, the canal was taken entirely out of Egyptian hands. This was done in spite of the fact that it passed through Egyptian territory, that Egyptian laborers had built it, and that a very large part of the money for the construction had been supplied by Egyptian rulers. Even the Khedive Ismail, for all his thoughtlessness and extravagance, understood the ambiguous nature of his country's position. He often said that he wanted the canal to belong to Egypt, not Egypt to the canal. Yet the country was to have no control of the canal, nor derive much profit from it, until 1956. When the first ship sailed through to Suez, the canal was already a pawn in an international game of politics. Two great powers—England and France —fought over it, and Egypt was the unhappy battleground of their struggle.

France, despite the fears of Great Britain, never really

137

Napoleon III is sent into exile toting on his back the remnants of his reign and dragging a ball and chain. Two hornlike wisps of hair sprout from either side of the visor of his jewel-encrusted cap.

succeeded in controlling the canal or dominating trade with the Far East. At the beginning she had every advantage. The administrative personnel of the company was French. Parts of Ismailia and Suez looked like French villages. And much of the company's stock was owned by Frenchmen. Yet for all this the French government itself played no significant part in the affairs of Egypt or in the operation of the canal. It did not because it could not.

The glories of the Second Empire had dissolved when on September 1, 1870, at the Battle of Sedan, Prussian forces crushed the French army and ended the short Franco-Prussian War. Napoleon III and the Empress Eugénie—less than a year after the opening ceremonies at Suez—were in exile, and the newly proclaimed Third Republic had troubles enough of its own without interfering in Middle Eastern affairs. Moreover, France had neither the navy nor the merchant ships to control the approaches to Suez or to make great use of the canal.

For England, the situation was far different. She was the most powerful nation in the world—with an impressive navy and a large merchant marine. Before long it was obvious that she was also the greatest beneficiary of de Lesseps' gift to the world. In the first year of operation, two thirds of the ships sailing through the canal were under the British flag. In succeeding years as much as 80 per cent of the total tonnage that passed between Port Said and Suez was British. Before long, Queen Victoria's ministers began to change their minds about the canal; the waterway had developed from an annoying French idea into a magnificent British asset. It was the new lifeline of empire. Now that the route around the Cape of Good Hope had become obsolete, the security of India and the freedom of British trade with the East depended upon the canal. British politicians realized that one way or another England had to control it. To risk having another nation in a position to bar British ships from the canal was unthinkable. So a quiet decision was made in London. It was only a question of waiting for the opportune moment.

The moment came in 1875. By that year the prodigal Ismail had succeeded in plunging his country hopelessly into debt. The Khedive's extravagant journey was almost over. He had borrowed to the limit, and European bankers were no longer willing to finance him—even at rates of interest that were approaching 20 per cent. Frantically he looked for a way out and saw that there was nothing left to pawn but his stock in the Suez Canal Company.

It was not long before Ismail's desperate plight came to the attention of the British Prime Minister, Benjamin Disraeli. This clever politician was well along in his program of glorifying the British Empire. He was soon, in fact, to have Victoria proclaimed Empress of India. The glamour of empire appealed greatly to Disraeli's romantic nature, but he was a practical politician as well. He saw in Ismail's need for money a way in which to secure the route to India and add immeasurably to the glory of the British Empire at the same time. The Khedive's predicament was an opportunity not to be missed. With possession of Ismail's stock, England would acquire a controlling interest in the Suez Canal. But Parliament was not in session, and there was no way he could get money from the treas-

Queen Victoria, proclaimed Empress of India in 1877, sits on an ornately carved ivory throne presented to her by an Indian rajah.

	Year	Number of Ships Passing Through	Net Transit Tonnage (Millions)	Passengers (Thousands)
SUEZ CANAL SHIPPING 1910-1964	1910	4,533	16.6	234
	1920	4,009	17.6	500
	1930	5,761	31.7	305
	1938	6,171	34.4	480
	1942	1,646	7.0	1
	1945	4,206	25.1	984
	1950	11,751	81.8	664
	1955	14,666	115.8	521
	1960	18,374	185.3	367
	1964	19,943	228.0	277

THE CANAL:
A CENTURY OF SERVICE

In the century since its 1869 opening, the Suez Canal has witnessed a steady increase in commercial traffic—with the exception of a decline during the World War II years (chart, bottom left). Today, tankers carrying oil from the Middle East represent the major part of the ship traffic; the decrease in passengers reflects the growth of commercial aviation. Although tonnage has increased almost fifteen-fold, revenues —going from $25,000,000 in 1910 to approximately $180,000,000 in 1964—increased by less than half that rate; the lesser growth was due mainly to steadily lowering rates. The larger draft of modern ships has necessitated the deepening and widening of the channel (chart at right), and new dredgers, like the modern suction dredger below, have been designed to speed up the process; the photograph at left, taken through a porthole, shows a convoy in transit.

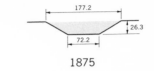

1875

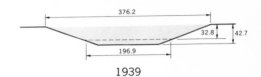

1939

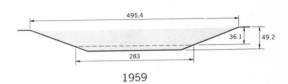

1959

All dimensions in feet

In a Punch *cartoon Disraeli ponders the question of how to use a key labeled "Suez Canal" that he has in his possession. The sphinx, guessing how Disraeli will solve the dilemma, winks knowingly.*

ury. He went ahead on his own responsibility. One evening, after discussing the matter with the Cabinet, he sent his private secretary to Baron Lionel Rothschild, England's leading banker.

Rothschild was finishing dinner when Disraeli's secretary arrived at his house. The secretary immediately explained that the Prime Minister needed 4,000,000 pounds ($20,000,000). The Baron was eating fruit and did not seem to be listening. He took time to peel several grapes with care, and then he spoke.

"What is your security?"

"The British government," replied Disraeli's emissary.

"You shall have it," said Rothschild, apparently absorbed in his dessert.

With this casual loan, made in Baron Rothschild's luxurious dining room, the story of England's involvement with the Suez Canal entered a new phase. Perhaps it is the most significant episode in the rich history of the British Empire. The purchase of Ismail's shares affected Britain's policy in Egypt and throughout the Middle East for years to come. Of all the outposts of her great empire the Suez Canal was the most important—and one of the last to be relinquished.

The Khedive ignored the political implications involved when he turned over 177,642 shares of the Suez Canal Company to the British Prime Minister. It was a dramatic moment, and Disraeli hurried to announce his triumph to Queen Victoria.

"It is just settled," he told her on November 25, 1875. "You have it, Madam."

For all the drama of Disraeli's *coup*, Britain won no great voice in the affairs of the canal. But she did have an impressive interest in it. It was true that she now owned more than 40 per cent of the Suez Canal Company; its bylaws, however, provided that no one shareholder could have more than ten votes.

Still, Britain's communications with the East remained vulnerable. The occupation of Egypt (and, therefore, of the canal) by a hostile power was a constant threat. A comprehensive solution had to be found, but England was forced to wait for the proper opportunity. When it came,

From 150 miles above the earth, the Gemini 4 spacecraft took this 1965 photograph of the fertile, fan-shaped Nile Delta and just beyond it the Suez Canal, stretching from the Mediterranean shore (left) to the Red Sea.

142

she sensed that she could solve the Egyptian question at last and assure the safety of British ships in the Suez Canal. It turned out to be a brutal, but effective, solution.

In 1882 a revolt broke out in Egypt. Under the guise of protecting the Khedive's government, England invaded. Alexandria was bombarded, warships entered the canal, and British soldiers occupied Port Said, Ismailia, and Suez. The French government protested the occupation as an act of aggression. De Lesseps himself rushed to the scene in an effort to remove the British from the canal zone, an area that he still regarded as his own domain. But he was an old man now, and his gesture was a futile one. The British put down the rebellion in a desert battle on September 13, 1882. This date marks the beginning of the British occupation of Egypt.

The English stayed in Egypt for almost seventy-five years. They stayed by using every political device they could command. Modern Egyptian history is an involved tapestry of British military governments, protectorates,

Egyptian soldiers, bayonets fixed, charge through the streets of Alexandria during the 1882 uprising.

144

puppet rulers, and varying Anglo-Egyptian treaties. There was a single purpose behind all this complex diplomacy: to secure the Suez Canal for England. Although still open to the ships of every nation, it came to be virtually a British possession. The French may have run the company, but the British had the canal. Even after England's official control of the Egyptian government ended in 1936, her troops still occupied a zone bordering, and including, the Suez Canal. In every part of the world it was a universally understood symbol of British imperialism. And it marked the measure of Britain's concern with the long lines of communication that led to and from her island kingdom.

President Nasser of the United Arab Republic announces the nationalization of the Suez Canal in a broadcast on July 26, 1956.

In the first half of the twentieth century, however, the world began to change, and England was forced to change with it. People talked of democracy and human rights, and the days of empire were drawing to a close. Inevitably, a time came when all that remained of Britain in Egypt was a handful of troops in the canal zone. At last a treaty was signed, and even this handful of soldiers left the Suez Canal in 1956.

By this date the nature of the Egyptian government had changed dramatically. King Farouk, the last royal ruler, had been exiled by a revolution of army officers in 1952. And one of these officers, Colonel Gamal Abdel Nasser, was now at the head of the government.

It was Nasser's ambition to establish an independent Egypt, free from all foreign influence, and to unite the whole Arab world under her banner. He has developed many projects for the improvement of the country, among them a great dam to be constructed at Aswan on the Upper Nile. When finished, it is expected to expand greatly Egypt's profitable cotton crop, irrigate two million acres of desert, and provide hydroelectric power for industry. It will cost well over a billion dollars.

After a series of involved negotiations it turned out that none of the great powers—neither Britain, France, the United States, nor the Soviet Union—would lend Nasser such a sum, although the Soviet Union ultimately provided extensive technical and financial assistance. Nasser was furious. He came to see the Suez Canal as his means of retaliation, as a way of acquiring the money necessary for the Aswan Dam and of removing all foreign influence from Egypt at the same time. He decided to seize the canal in the name of his government.

On Thursday, July 26, 1956 (the fourth anniversary of the Egyptian revolution), Nasser gave a speech about the

The sky above the canal zone fills with French paratroopers during the 1956 Franco-British attempt to take over control of the canal.

history of Egypt under foreign rule and emphasized the country's present freedom. While he spoke, squads of Egyptian soldiers with drawn guns took over the offices of the Suez Canal Company in Cairo. At the same time other troops were occupying Port Said, Ismailia, and Suez. Since the last of the British garrison had left in May, the canal was defenseless. Egyptians assumed all the positions of authority, and the French, with no means of defending themselves, were forced to leave. The Suez Canal Company no longer existed. Nasser's move was a brilliant and dramatic one, and the canal belonged to Egypt at last.

France and Britain were enraged. Britain, in particular, saw Nasser's action as justification for an attempt to regain her control of Suez. The habit of empire was a hard one to break, and she was waiting for an excuse to reoccupy Suez. That excuse came sooner than expected. And it came from Israel.

Israel and Egypt had been antagonistic neighbors for the seven years following the Arab-Israeli war of 1948–49 in which the Jewish state had won its independence. Border raids between the two countries were daily events, and Israeli ships had long been barred from using the Suez Canal. At the end of October, 1956, the situation exploded. The Israeli government, feeling provoked to the limit, sent troops across the Egyptian border on the Sinai Peninsula. These troops moved quickly in the direction of the Suez Canal.

Britain and France had been having difficulty in setting up an international committee to operate the canal and put an end to Nasser's control of it. But now, with the Israeli invasion of Egypt threatening the canal, they found an excuse for immediate and decisive action. Both countries expressed concern over the fact that the great waterway might become a combat area. They decided to act quickly.

On November 5, 1956, French and British paratroopers landed at Ismailia and set about occupying the whole length of the canal. They came, their governments said, to protect the interests of international shipping. The Egyptians were soon routed, and the canal was under Anglo-French control.

This European intervention in Egyptian affairs, though successful from a military point of view, was a political disaster. It soon brought the whole world to the edge of a general conflict. ‚The strategic importance of the Suez Canal was so great that the Soviet Union became involved, as did the United States. The crisis lasted for two more

The Pollux, *one of fourteen ships sunk in November, 1956, to block canal traffic, rests on her port side in the harbor of Port Said.*

days. Finally, under pressure from the United States, the United Nations was called in to settle the dispute. A cease-fire was declared, and the British and the French were ordered to withdraw from the canal zone. The withdrawal was a humiliating one, and the United Nations subsequently decided that the Suez Canal did in fact belong to Nasser.

(Ships sunk in the channel by the Egyptians during the brief hostilities of November, 1956, temporarily blocked the Suez Canal to all traffic. Under United Nations auspices, the waterway was cleared and reopened by January, 1957.)

Today, the Egyptians are masters of the canal. In order to hold it legally they have paid a large indemnity to the Suez Canal Company. Now called the Compagnie Financière de Suez, it is simply a French investment enterprise with no further interest in the canal. (Among the company's current projects is a proposed tunnel under the English Channel.) The Egyptian government made the last pay-

Dynamite, placed by a member of an Egyptian mob (top), destroys the de Lesseps statue at Port Said.

ment to its shareholders on January 1, 1963. Neither the French nor the British have any further business at Suez.

Yet the Suez Canal itself, in spite of its new ownership, is still international in character. Reports indicate that it is running as smoothly as ever. In fact, a writer for the New York *Times* said in the spring of 1965 that the canal "has become a model of Egyptian efficiency, with constantly improving facilities and rising revenue." Nasser's plan, now in operation, calls for deepening the canal and doubling its width, among other improvements.

It is curious, now that the French and the British are no longer involved in its operation, that the canal has returned to de Lesseps' original concept of it. He never wanted it to be a diplomatic pawn or a battleground for politicians. He thought of it simply as a gift to the world— as a path of trade and communication open to all nations.

Ironically, few Egyptians have understood the sincere motives that guided de Lesseps in the creation of the Suez Canal. His name has been a hated one in Egypt. Quite unjustly, it has come to stand for all the abuses of colonialism and foreign occupation. His very name, in fact, was the signal used by Nasser to set the seizure of the canal in operation on July 26, 1956. And five months later, on the day before Christmas, when the French and the British had left Suez for good, a wild mob of Egyptians swarmed through Port Said, eager to destroy any last signs of foreign influence. Some of the mob found dynamite and, after three attempts, managed to blow up the huge bronze statue of de Lesseps that dominated the harbor and marked the entrance to the canal. Fragments of the eighty-foot statue fell smoking into the water.

But this violent gesture did not destroy the work of Ferdinand de Lesseps, who had died in 1894 at the age of eighty-nine. It did not put an end to the great adventure that had begun in Alexandria in 1832. No mob could destroy the magnitude of the accomplishment.

The canal still cuts through the desert, there are flowers at Ismailia, and two worlds are securely—if uneasily— bound together. Ferdinand de Lesseps is gone, and his great statue is gone. But the words once inscribed on its base shine in every drop of water flowing through the sand from Port Said to Suez: *Aperire terram gentibus.*

A bullet-riddled window in the Port Said lighthouse (opposite)—souvenir of the 1956 crisis—offers a view of the first ship through the reopened canal.

AMERICAN HERITAGE
PUBLISHING CO., INC.

James Parton, *President*
Joseph J. Thorndike, *Editor in Chief*
Richard M. Ketchum, *Editorial Director, Book Division*
Stephen W. Sears, *Editor, Education Department*
Irwin Glusker, *Art Director*

HORIZON CARAVEL BOOKS

JOSEPH L. GARDNER, *Managing Editor*
Janet Czarnetzki, *Art Director*
Elaine K. Andrews, *Copy Editor*
Mary Sherman Parsons, *Picture Editor*
Nancy Simon, *Editorial Researcher*
Gertrudis Feliu, *Chief, European Bureau*
Claire de Forbin, *European Bureau*

ACKNOWLEDGMENTS

The Editors are particularly grateful for the generous cooperation of the Direction Generale, Library and Phototheque of the Compagnie Financière de Suez in Paris. In addition they would like to thank the following individuals:

Giselle de La Bégassiere
Bernard Bothmer, Brooklyn Museum
Professor G. Cervani, Trieste, author of *Voyage en Egypte de Pasquale Revoltella*
Sophie Ebeid, Cairo
Ahmed Fouad, Deputy Director of Public Relations, Suez Canal Authority, Ismailia
Mrs. Mary Jenkins, London
Safynaz Kazem, Arab Information Center, New York
Countess Mathieu de Lesseps
Count Pierre de Lesseps
Count Roland de Lesseps, Paris
Mrs. Tauni de Lesseps, Greenwich, Connecticut
B. Naudin, Musée de Chateauroux
Carl Raswan, Santa Barbara, California
Maps by Argenziano Associates

150

Ferries and lateen-rigged vessels transporting goods and passengers ply the busy Nile.

FURTHER READING

For those who wish to read more about Egypt and the Suez Canal, the following books are recommended:

Aldred, Cyril, *The Egyptians*. Praeger, 1961.

Beatty, Charles, *De Lesseps of Egypt*. Harper, 1956.

Crabites, Pierre, *Ismail, the Maligned Khedive*. London, 1933.

Crabites, Pierre, *The Spoliation of the Suez*. London, 1940.

De Lesseps, Ferdinand, *Recollection of Forty Years*. New York, 1888.

Halevy, Elie, *History of the English People in the Nineteenth Century*. Vol. IV. Ernest Benn, Ltd., 1951.

Hallberg, Charles W., *The Suez Canal*. Columbia University Press, 1931.

Herold, J. Christopher, *Bonaparte in Egypt*. Harper & Row, 1962.

Jarvis, H. Wood, *Pharaoh to Farouk*. New York, 1955.

Marlowe, John, *A History of Modern Egypt and Anglo-Egyptian Relations, 1800–1953*. Praeger, 1954.

Marlowe, John, *World Ditch*. Macmillan, 1964.

Maurois, André, *Disraeli*. London, 1927.

Moorehead, Alan, *The Blue Nile*. Dell, 1962.

Payne, Robert, *The Canal Builders*. Macmillan, 1959.

Posener, Georges, *Dictionary of Egyptian Civilization*. Tudor, 1959.

Schoenfield, Hugh J., *Ferdinand de Lesseps*. London, 1937.

Schoenfield, Hugh J., *The Suez Canal*. London, 1940.

Siegfried, André, *Suez and Panama*. New York, 1940.

Robertson, Terence, *Crisis*. New York, 1965.

Trevelyan, G. M., *Illustrated English Social History*. Vol. IV. Longmans, Green, 1952.

Williams, Roger L., *The World of Napoleon III*. Collier Books, 1962.

INDEX

Bold face indicates pages on which maps or illustrations appear